Cultural and Creative Industries in the Western Balkans

Cultural and Creative Industries in the Western Balkans is a book that explores the dynamic and evolving landscape of the cultural policy, cultural and creative industries (CCI) across the region. This book examines the unique positioning of CCIs, their role in preserving cultural expression and content, and their economic impact on these societies, all within the framework of social, political, and economic trends and transformations in the region. Each chapter investigates various themes, including the unique perspective on the Western Balkans (WB), the development of cultural policies, the current state of the CCIs and their economic impact, the challenges specific to each country, and the future prospects of this sector.

Through data-driven insights, the book offers readers an in-depth look at the relationship between creativity and policy, showcasing how the WB region is preserving and developing its CCIs.

Professionals, academics, and policymakers can benefit from the book's relevant recommendations for strengthening CCI ecosystems in the WB. This shortform book is the first to provide an expert overview of the cultural and creative sectors in the WB and will be valuable reading for researchers and advanced students of the creative industries, global cultural policy, and Eastern Europe more broadly.

Violeta Simjanovska brings over 25 years of global experience in arts management and cultural policy. Her career, which began in electrical engineering, evolved into managing a music festival and leading a performing arts research centre as general manager. She has initiated and led numerous international projects, with expertise in CCI, and the relationship between arts and society.

As a researcher, Dr. Simjanovska has led over 20 international research initiatives and has published more than 50 articles and books on arts management, CCI, and arts-related societal issues. Her research contributions have significantly advanced understanding in these fields, driving forward innovative practices in arts management and cultural policy.

Her professional footprint includes more than 30 countries, with key focus areas including cultural policy, CCI, arts management, intercultural competences, and strategic management and leadership. At the moment, Dr. Simjanovska works as Head of the Arts Management Department at Sibelius Academy, University of the Arts Helsinki. She is also a cultural consultant for the United Nations Educational, Scientific and Cultural Organization (UNESCO), the European Commission, and the British Council. Her academic contributions extend to institutions such as Goldsmiths, University of London, the University of Belgrade, and the Music Academy in Brno. From 2022 to 2024, she was a member of the Executive Board of the European Network of Cultural Administration Training Centres (ENCATC), Europe's leading network on cultural management and policy.

Routledge Focus on the Global Creative Economy

Series Editor: Aleksandar Brkić

Goldsmiths, University of London, UK

This innovative Shortform book series aims to provoke and inspire new ways of thinking, new interpretations, emerging research, and insights from different fields. In rethinking the relationship of creative economies and societies beyond the traditional frameworks, the series is intentionally inclusive. Featuring diverse voices from around the world, books in the series bridge scholarship and practice across arts and cultural management, the creative industries and the global creative economy.

Climate Change and the Creative Economy in India
Disadvantaged, Disturbed and Dislocated Indian Weavers
Pragya Sharma

Research, Development and Innovation in the Creative Industries
Reframing Our Understanding of the Creative Economy
Ruxandra Lupu, Marlen Komorowski, Justin Lewis and Máté Miklos Fodor

Achieving Creative Justice in the U.S. Creative Sector
antonio c. cuyler

Caribbean Industries in Culture
Developing Sustainable Actions for the Creative Ecology
Suzanne Burke

Cultural and Creative Industries in the Western Balkans
Violeta Simjanovska

For more information about this series, please visit: www.routledge.com/Routledge-Focus-on-the-Global-Creative-Economy/book-series/RFGCE

Cultural and Creative Industries in the Western Balkans

Violeta Simjanovska

Routledge
Taylor & Francis Group
LONDON AND NEW YORK

First published 2026
by Routledge
4 Park Square, Milton Park, Abingdon, Oxon OX14 4RN

and by Routledge
605 Third Avenue, New York, NY 10158

Routledge is an imprint of the Taylor & Francis Group, an informa business

British Library Cataloguing-in-Publication Data
A catalogue record for this book is available from the British Library

ISBN: 978-1-032-72456-0 (hbk)
ISBN: 978-1-032-72468-3 (pbk)
ISBN: 978-1-032-72466-9 (ebk)

DOI: 10.4324/9781032724669

Typeset in Times New Roman
by Apex CoVantage, LLC

This work is dedicated to my daughter Aya and my husband Vuk, for their unwavering support, and to all those who continue to inspire me.

Contents

Preface

This book has emerged from more than 25 years of my personal journey in the arts and cultural field, primarily in the Balkans, but also working in Europe, the USA, Africa, and Australia. Over the course of this time, I have had the privilege of leading more than 100 international projects and programmes while also contributing to the creation of cultural policy at both national and local levels in the region. My involvement has extended in the research field, formal and non-formal education within the creative sector, and active participation in various European Commission programmes. Moreover, I have served as an expert and evaluator of numerous initiatives, shaping the course of these creative endeavours.

This work is a distillation of the extensive experience and insights I have acquired regarding the cultural and creative industries (CCI) in the Western Balkans over the past 25 years. Importantly, my last seven years of living and working in Finland have afforded me a critical view through which to reflect upon the concepts surrounding creative industries, particularly their contextualisation (or lack thereof) within the Western Balkans. This shift in perspective has illuminated the profound impact these industries have, or could have, on local communities.

Writing this book has been far from an easy journey. One of the significant challenges I faced was the limitation of existing data on the CCI sector, which influenced the overall content. Additionally, during this period, I encountered several difficulties in my personal life, related to my closest persons, which made the writing process especially difficult. However, despite these obstacles, I am glad of what this book represents, a significant marker for the CCI sector in the Western Balkans, offering a historic overview and forward-looking perspective on its future possibilities.

Acknowledgements

This book has been prepared with important and warm support from many individuals and organisations.

I would like to express my deepest gratitude to my husband, who supported me throughout the entire process and helped with some technical issues related to the book; to my daughter, who understood why I couldn't spend time with her while I was writing; to Tulay Tahir for her feedback and support during the writing process; to my proofreader, Ida Blazevska; to my superior at Sibelius Academy, Tuuli Talvitie, for her understanding; and to Bojana Colović and Bojana Ristić for their support. I am also thankful to all my friends and colleagues who provided valuable information, critical opinions, reflections, and thoughts on the topics and subjects presented in this book.

I also extend my thanks to everyone who, in any way, helped me complete this work.

Finally, I would like to acknowledge those who granted permission to use their data: David Throsby, Rahman Nurković, Mimoza Petrevska, Jelena Vasić, PhD Chamber of Commerce and Industry Serbia, Institute for Entrepreneurship and Economic Development Montenegro, Eurostat, State Statistical Office North Macedonia, UNCTAD, World Bank, OXO, ODA Theatre, and Art House and Film Institute Montenegro.

In the preparation of this book, I made meaningful and responsible use of AI to support and enhance the writing process. Specifically, I used Chat GPT-4 and QuillBot to assist with translating selected sections from Macedonian, Serbian, Finnish, and Albanian into English. These tools were also used for proofreading, grammar checking, paraphrasing, and rewording while maintaining the integrity and originality of the content, which remains entirely mine. Additionally, I utilised Zotero for managing and formatting references, particularly in applying APA citation style throughout various parts of the text.

Introduction

About the (Western) Balkan

If the Balkans hadn't existed, they would have been invented.
(Keyserling, 1925, as cited in Todorova, 1997)

Writing about the Western Balkans is not a simple task. The geographical scope is the simplest aspect of this region, which usually includes Albania, Bosnia and Herzegovina, Bulgaria, Croatia, Greece, Kosovo, Montenegro, North Macedonia, Romania, Serbia, and Slovenia (See Figure 0.1). According to Todorova (2009), the most important and complex aspects of understanding the Balkans are historical and cultural, internal and external relations, and interactions. Precisely, these relationships have shaped from one side the identities of these countries and from the other their perception of the region.

This region has historically been viewed as a crossroad between East and West. It has also been seen as a region marked by centuries of conflicts and divisions, which contributes to the captioning of the region as a "Powder keg" of Europe. In the historical context in relation to the West, the Balkans has a specific place, and it has always been problematic in terms of its understanding, interpretations, and narratives.

The Balkans have historically been influenced not only by the West but equally, if not more profoundly, by the East. For several centuries, the region was under the domination of the Ottoman Empire, which left lasting cultural, social, religious, and institutional legacies (Sugar, 1977; Todorova, 2009). The Ottoman influence introduced Islamic traditions, Ottoman law, architectural styles, administrative structures, and patterns of landholding that distinguished the Balkans from Western Europe.

Beyond Ottoman rule, another powerful Eastern influence came from Russia, which positioned itself as a guardian of Orthodox Christian communities in the Balkans (Bideleux & Jeffries, 2007). The Russian Orthodox Church was instrumental in strengthening religious and cultural ties with the Slavic nations, such as Serbia, Montenegro, North Macedonia, Bulgaria, and

DOI: 10.4324/9781032724669-1

Figure 0.1 Map of the Western Balkans

Source: Google Map

Romania. Russia's Pan-Slavic ideology, promoted from the nineteenth century onwards, encouraged the notion of shared Slavic brotherhood (Roudometof, 2001). Additionally, the Eastern Orthodox Church, centred historically in Constantinople (later Istanbul), shaped the spiritual and cultural identities of many Balkan communities.

Alongside these influences, the Austro-Hungarian Empire's presence in the northwestern parts of the Balkans brought a different, Central European model of governance and culture, creating a complex layering of Eastern and Western influences. Thus, rather than serving as a simple boundary line between East and West, the Balkans historically functioned as a hybrid cultural zone, where Eastern and Western civilisational influences merged, clashed, and evolved over centuries (Đokić, 2023; Jović, 2009).

This dual legacy, Eastern and Western, continues to define the region's cultural complexity, internal diversity, and external perceptions. Todorova portrays the Balkans as historically complicated with both Eastern and Western influences, where the Ottoman past has significantly shaped the region's cultural and social landscape and perspectives. Despite the Ottoman orientation towards the West, its Eastern cultural affiliations prevented the Balkans from fully integrating into the Western narrative, thus maintaining a unique in-between identity. This dual affiliation challenges the simplistic understanding of East versus

West, illustrating a common relationship that has made a strong imprint on the Balkan identity. This persisting legacy complicates modern perceptions of the Balkans within Europe, suggesting a region marked by a rich, yet conflicted, history that crosses cultural and geopolitical divides (Todorova, 2009).

Many scholars have problematised the relation between East and West and, in particular, the clear distinction between the two, emphasising the "otherness" of the Balkans and analysing it from different angles, such as historical influences, cultural perceptions, ethnicity, race, gender, narratives, and the role of Europe (later the European Union) in shaping the region's identity and politics (Glenny, 2012; Goldsworthy, 1998; Baker, 2018; Žižek & Horvat, 2014; Todorova, 2009). Although the Balkan region was not formally colonised in the classical sense of overseas colonialism, the centuries-long rule under the Ottoman Empire and later the Austro-Hungarian Empire bore many characteristics similar to colonial domination, particularly regarding political control, economic exploitation, and cultural imposition (Đokić, 2023; Jović, 2009). The experiences of subordination and external rule shaped the social, cultural, and political dynamics of the region profoundly, producing legacies comparable to those seen in formally colonised regions of the world. The hierarchical framing came not only in political and economic forms but also through cultural imperialism, where the Balkans were often portrayed as less civilised and needing Western intervention or guidance. This portrayal aligns with Edward Said's concept of Orientalism, which Todorova adapts into her analysis, positioning the Balkans within a similar framework where Eastern Europe is constructed as inferior to the West (Said, 1978).

Further, in "Imagining the Balkans," Todorova (2009) gives a clear picture of how the Balkans have been stereotyped and viewed through the "western" lens. The same author critiques Western perceptions that have historically portrayed the Balkans as the "Other" of Europe, a region characterised by barbarism and tribalism, which has been a persistent stereotype within Western discourse. She further argues that this stereotype of the Balkans as a turbulent and backward region has been both an oversimplified generalisation and a form of cultural discrimination that neglect the rich and complex histories of the Balkan peoples. These stereotypes have further influenced the perception of the Balkans and the internal dynamics of the region. The tendency of stereotyping and the perceived need to "civilise" the Balkans from the West have had deep and lasting impacts, affecting how Balkan societies have been viewed with their historical narratives (Todorova, 2009).

As an echo to the Western stereotypes, the intellectuals from the Balkans tried to build different narratives. The great Macedonian writer Goran Stefanovski looks at the Balkans as a metaphor for a labyrinth at the heart of Europe. In one of his interviews, he stated:

> You cannot ask me not to feel like a part of the deepest and oldest world, when Heraclea is my home, when Ohrid is my home, when Via Ignatia, the

> only highway that existed in Europe between the 5th and 15th centuries, passed by my grandmother's house in Bitola. Everything cannot be with you, and nothing with us!
>
> (Petrevska, 2009)

With this statement, Stefanovski describes the Balkans not just as a geographical region but as a complex emotional and historical space within the broader European context. He further criticised the Western perception of the Balkans, underlining the rich history, strong education, creativity and intellects that exist in this area, suggesting the Balkans as crossroads of cultures and creativity. He employs Ohrid, a city in North Macedonia situated along the oldest lake in Europe, renowned for its historical significance in the development of the Cyrillic alphabet and Glagolitic script. He also references Heraclea, an ancient city located two kilometres from Bitola, North Macedonia, founded in the mid-fourth century BC. This city played a crucial role as a strategic centre in the region for over a millennium. Additionally, Stefanovski calls upon the symbolism of Via Egnatia, an ancient road that connected the East and West, using these geographical and historical elements to metaphorically highlight the crossroads of Eastern and Western influences that have shaped the identity of the Balkan Peninsula over the centuries. Via Egnatia, in Stefanovski's context, serves as an emotional symbol for the paths of cultural and historical currents that flow through the Balkans, influencing its people and their narratives. He suggested that this road, much like the modern Balkans, has been a route of continuous movement and exchange, witnessing the comings and goings of various empires, armies, ideas, and cultures. This historical perspective gives a deep sense of the place and the complexities of Balkan identity, caught between the forces of past empires and modern nationalistic drives.

Inseparable from Europe, however, the Balkan countries have been framed as "internally different" from a cultural point of view, a concept discussed by scholars such as Todorova (2009) and Roudometof (2001), and this perception has been present in academic as well as in daily political, socioeconomic, and cultural discourses throughout history. The complex relations between the Balkans and the other parts of Europe have significantly shaped the construction of what scholars describe as a layered, evolving, and often contested Balkan identity (Todorova, 2009; Roudometof, 2001; Verdery, 1996; Štiks, 2015; Stojanović, 2010; Đokić, 2012; Brkić, 2012; Subotić, 2011; Pavlowitch, 1999; Hatzopoulos, 2008; Gori & Ivanova, 2017; Öztürk, 2021; Kolozova, 2004). This identity is manifested across all spheres of society, from political discourse to cultural production and everyday practices, and remains a subject of ongoing scholarly inquiry. It continues to be shaped by historical legacies, post-socialist transformations, regional narratives, processes of Europeanisation, and contemporary geopolitical developments.

The Rise of New Orders: Yugoslavia's Federation and Albania's Isolation After WWII

After World War II, the Balkans witnessed significant geopolitical transformations, most notably the formation of socialist Yugoslavia and the establishment of communist Albania. These changes reflected broader shifts in Eastern Europe, as countries realigned with emerging global powers and ideologies. Yugoslavia was unique in its approach to managing the diverse ethnic and national identities within its borders, a complexity extensively analysed by historians such as Jović (2009), Calić (2019), and Pavlowitch (1999). Their works illustrate how Yugoslavia's federal structure attempted to balance ethnic plurality with overarching unity, though underlying tensions persisted beneath the surface. The country was organised as a federation of six republics: Bosnia and Herzegovina, Croatia, Macedonia, Montenegro, Serbia, and Slovenia. Two autonomous provinces, Kosovo and Vojvodina, were also created within Serbia. The leader of this federation was Josip Broz Tito, where he created a unique path of non-alignment and worker-orientated and managed socialism, known as Titoism. This new set up diverged from the Soviet model and positioned Yugoslavia in a prominent role in global affairs, particularly within the Non-Aligned Movement (Lampe, 2000; Banac, 1988). The governance of the country differed significantly from other communist states, beyond its shared ideology, through greater openness to international engagement, allowing unrestricted travel and embracing Western influences in education and culture. Despite this relative liberalism compared to other Eastern Bloc countries, the state continued to exert ideological control over cultural production and consumption.

In contrast, Albania, under Enver Hoxha's leadership, established a People's Republic marked by extreme isolationism and widespread admiration for the leader's personality (Hoxha, 1982). Initially aligned with Yugoslavia, and later with the Soviet Union, Albania later turned to China for support following the Tito-Stalin split (Biberaj, 2019). Hoxha's regime implemented strict state controls and severe restrictions on foreign influences, creating a repressive and isolated state (Prifti, 1978).

The legacies of these divergent systems profoundly shaped the region. Yugoslavia's ethno-federal model and Albania's isolationist policies influenced the political dynamics of the Balkans well beyond the fall of Communism.

A Region in Transition: Between the Yugoslav Wars and Albania's Awakening in the 1990s

Yugoslavia's breakdown in the 1990s and Albania's gradual opening were both rooted in the historical paths established in the post-WWII period (Judah, 1997). The complex and long-standing factors contributing to Yugoslavia's conflicts of the 1990s are perfectly illustrated in the works of Glenny (2012),

Jović (2009), Calić (2019), Đokić (2012), Markovina (2015), who emphasise that the breakup of this country was not merely a result of one single reason; it encompassed the ancient ethnic hatreds, political ideology and manipulation, and international miscalculations. In his comprehensive analysis *The Balkans: Nationalism, War, and the Great Powers*, 1804–2012, Glenny (2012) examines the complex and enduring factors that contributed to the Balkan conflicts of the 1990s, identifying historical, nationalistic, and geopolitical tensions as primary catalysts for the region's persistent instability and turbulence. He points out that the fragmentation of Yugoslavia resulted not only from internal divisions but was significantly shaped by international influences. Nationalism played a crucial role, as regional leaders manipulated ethnic divisions and historical hatred to push their citizens to conflict. Furthermore, he critiques the global and, particularly, EU community's ineffective response to this conflict, attributing part of the blame to their inadequate perception of the Balkans' intricate historical and cultural landscape. He highlights the severe human suffering resulting from these conflicts and challenges the oversimplified narratives that frequently dominate global discussions about the Balkans.

Similarly, Gottfried Wagner, an Austrian who served as the CEO of the European Cultural Foundation in Amsterdam in *The Heart of the Matter* (Keulemans & Cameron, 2006), critically addresses the dangerous perception of the Balkans in the 1990s as an isolated and troubled region distinct from the rest of Europe. He discusses how this notion was historically reinforced by European superpowers that contributed to creating a "Balkan problem" through mechanisms of exclusion and ignorance, influenced by the rise of "Mitteleuropa" ideologists. Reflecting on his personal experiences and sensitivities as both a "sceptical Austrian" and a "hopeful European," Wagner acknowledges the EU's mixed responses to the region's crises, including its slow reaction to the warning signs of conflict and nationalism that led to wars and genocide (Keulemans & Cameron, 2006). Despite these challenges, he praises the remarkable individuals from the Balkans, such as activists, artists, educators, and intellectuals from countries like Albania, Bosnia and Herzegovina, Croatia, North Macedonia, Montenegro, Kosovo, and Serbia, for their passionate advocacy for peace, reconciliation, and democratic values. Impressed by the resilience of these people and intellectual passion, Wagner called on his peers in the EU to learn from, and collaborate with, these influential figures to better understand and support the region's rich cultural and human potential. Unfortunately, this kind of understanding of the Balkan region did not resonate strongly within the EU institutions at that time.

While Yugoslavia's disintegration in the 1990s was marked by violent conflicts and ethno-nationalist fragmentation, Albania's trajectory during the same period reflected a gradual and complex opening to the outside world. Following decades of extreme isolationism under Enver Hoxha's regime, which severed ties first with Yugoslavia, then the Soviet Union, and finally China, Albania entered the post-Cold War era deeply marginalised within

Europe (Biberaj, 2019; Prifti, 1978). The authoritarian structures established in the post-war period entrenched a centralised system that collapsed rapidly after Hoxha's death and the subsequent weakening of the Party of Labour of Albania. As Judah (1997) emphasises, Albania's delayed and cautious re-engagement with the international community in the 1990s was a direct consequence of its historical trajectory, characterised by deep mistrust of external influences and a highly controlled internal political culture. Economic hardship, political unrest, and the collapse of state institutions culminated in the 1997 crisis, highlighting the fragile nature of Albania's transition (Glenny, 2012). Despite these challenges, Albania gradually embarked on reforms, initiated democratisation processes, and sought integration with Euro-Atlantic structures, signalling a profound, if turbulent, shift from its isolationist past towards a European future (European Commission, n.d.).

Redefining the Balkans: European Union Aspirations After Conflict and Transition

After the war in Yugoslavia and after the fall of the regime in Albania, the European Union integration process of the region has started, marking significant political, economic, social, and cultural changes. The concept of "Europeanisation" in the context of the former Yugoslav countries and the wider Balkans generally refers to the transformation processes these countries undergo to align more closely with EU policies, practices, and standards (Zimmermann & Jakir, 2015). This process includes adopting EU legislation, norms, and values, which often requires significant changes in national legislation and policy practices.

Various forms of regional cooperation were also promoted to facilitate economic integration and reconciliation. An important point in the process of European integration of these countries was the Stabilisation and Association Process (SAP), initiated in June 1999, mainly focused on supporting these countries in this transition period and faster EU integration process (European Commission, n.d.).

Another significant framework in this context is the Central European Free Trade Agreement (CEFTA), which the Balkan countries joined after 2006, fostering trade liberalisation and economic collaboration (CEFTA Secretariat, n.d.). Despite the political tensions, CEFTA has provided one of the most stable and practical platforms for regional cooperation, particularly in the field of trade.

In this process of transformation, Slovenia became the first former Yugoslavian country to join the European Union in 2004. Its transition was shaped by a combination of domestic reforms and compliance with EU standards, which facilitated a smoother integration process. Slovenia's entry into the EU was seen as a culmination of its Western orientation (Zimmermann & Jakir, 2015). Croatia joined the EU later, in 2013, after a long negotiation period marked by various reforms in the judiciary, economy, and anti-corruption measures. The EU accession was viewed within Croatia as a strategic goal that would stabilise the country, economically and politically, by establishing it in European institutions (Maldini & Pauković, 2015).

Formation of Western Balkans as a Political Construct

After Slovenia and Croatia joined the European Union, the term "Western Balkans" began to take shape, primarily as a political construct. It refers to six countries: Albania, Bosnia and Herzegovina, Kosovo, Montenegro, North Macedonia, and Serbia, five of which were former republics of the Socialist Federal Republic of Yugoslavia (SFRY). These nations have been, and continue to be, in various stages of the EU accession process. The term was popularised in the 1990s as a way to distinguish these countries from the broader Balkan Peninsula and from the EU member states within the region, namely Greece, Slovenia, Bulgaria, Romania, and Croatia. This construct was primarily used by the US and European policymakers (Helvetas, 2018).

The integration of the Western Balkan countries into the European Union has been and still is on varying trajectories, as mentioned before, each influenced by their unique national contexts and the broader geopolitical landscape. Reforms in different fields, such as education, justice, culture, health, and administration, which were advocated for decades ago, are still not fully implemented, partly due to political instability and structural limitations.

In 2014, the Berlin Process was initiated and designed to accelerate EU integration by promoting regional cooperation and resolving long-standing bilateral issues, and also with large financial assistance from EU funds. However, Marku and Teqja (2024) argue that the process has been slow and stagnating and has not significantly advanced the EU integration agenda due to unsolved political, territorial, and economic persistent challenges.

The European Union integration process in the Western Balkans has been characterised by a continuous struggle between pro-European reformers and authoritarian hybrid regimes, as highlighted by Bieber and Tzifakis (2019). Moreover, the growing influence of Russia and China across various sectors in the region has further complicated the dynamics, prompting renewed attention and strategic engagement from the European Union.

Another challenge in this process, as Belloni R. and Brunazzo M. (2017) are indicating, is the "enlargement fatigue" the European Union has been experiencing in the last years, mainly because of the economic crises in 2008, the financial and political crisis in Europe, and the post-2016 "Brexit" situation. In addition, the COVID-19 crisis, Ukraine war and recently the Israeli–Palestinian conflict also influenced this process, along with the changing priorities within the EU, shaken by the changes in world geo-politics. The authors also highlight a significant version of EU integration fatigue evident in Western Balkan nations, where varying degrees of Euroscepticism have been arising.

It has emerged as a significant political and cultural phenomenon, reflecting broader trends seen across Europe, but with unique regional characteristics.

Regarding the current state, the integration of the Western Balkans into the EU has seen mixed progress. Some countries, like Montenegro, Serbia, and Albania, have advanced in their negotiation chapters, while others, like North Macedonia, Bosnia and Herzegovina, and Kosovo, are in different phases in this process, mainly stagnating within it. The path to EU membership, as it is mentioned before, is often complicated by issues such as political instability, economic vulnerabilities, geopolitical changes, and unresolved disagreements.

In conclusion, the integration of the Western Balkans into the EU remains an ongoing journey marked by significant challenges and achievements. The success of these efforts will depend largely on the political will of the governments and their ability to implement necessary reforms. From the other side, the EU's readiness to accommodate new members, despite the internal and external pressures, will play a crucial role.

References

Baker, C. (2018). *Race and the Yugoslav region: Postsocialist, post-conflict, postcolonial?* Manchester University Press.

Banac, I. (1988). *With Stalin against Tito: Cominformist splits in Yugoslav communism*. Cornell University Press.

Belloni, R., & Brunazzo, M. (2017). After "brexit": The Western Balkans in the European waiting room. *European Review of International Studies*, *4*(1), 21–38.

Biberaj, E. (2019). *Albania in transition: The rocky road to democracy*. Routledge.

Bideleux, R., & Jeffries, I. (2007). *The Balkans: A post-communist history*. Routledge.

Bieber, F., & Tzifakis, N. (Eds.). (2019). *The Western Balkans in the world: Linkages and relations with non-Western countries*. Routledge.

Brkić, A. (2012). *Cultural policy frameworks: (Re)constructing national and supranational identities: The Balkans and the European Union*. European Cultural Foundation. https://www.researchgate.net/publication/318702002_Cultural_policy_frameworks_Reconstructing_national_and_supranational_identities_The_Balkans_and_the_European_Union

Calić, M.-J. (2019). *A history of Yugoslavia*. Purdue University Press.

CEFTA Secretariat. (n.d.). *About CEFTA*. https://cefta.int/

Đokić, D. (2012). Nationalism, myth and reinterpretation of history: The neglected case of interwar Yugoslavia. *European History Quarterly*, *42*(1), 71–95. https://doi.org/10.1177/0265691411428532

Đokić, D. (2023). *A concise history of Serbia*. Cambridge University Press.

European Commission. (n.d.). Stabilisation and association process. *Neighbourhood and Enlargement*. https://neighbourhood-enlargement.ec.europa.eu/enlargement-policy/glossary/stabilisation-and-association-process_en

Glenny, M. (2012). *The Balkans: Nationalism, war, and the great powers, 1804–2012* (New and updated ed.). House of Anansi.

Goldsworthy, V. (1998). *Inventing Ruritania: The imperialism of the imagination*. Yale University Press.

Gori, M., & Ivanova, M. (Eds.). (2017). *Balkan dialogues: Negotiating identity between prehistory and the present*. Routledge.

Hatzopoulos, P. (2008). *The Balkans beyond nationalism and identity: International relations and ideology*. I.B. Tauris.

Helvetas. (2018, September). *Labeling the Balkans*. Helvetas. https://www.helvetas.org/en/eastern-europe/about-us/follow-us/helvetas-mosaic/article/September2018/Labeling-the-Balkans

Hoxha, E. (1982). *Address to the electors*. Nentori Publishing House.

Jović, D. (2009). *Yugoslavia: A state that withered away*. Purdue University Press.

Judah, T. (1997). *The Serbs: History, myth, and the destruction of Yugoslavia*. Yale University Press.

Keulemans, C., & Cameron, D. (Eds.). (2006). *The heart of the matter: The role of the arts and culture in the Balkans' European integration*. European Cultural Foundation.

Keyserling, H. (1925). *The travel diary of a philosopher*. Harcourt, Brace & Company.

Keyserling, H. (1928). *Europe*. Harcourt, Brace & Company.

Kolozova, K. (2004). The grain of the real within the identity. *Identities: Journal for Politics, Gender and Culture*, *3*(1), 9–27. Research Center in Gender Studies – Skopje & Euro-Balkan Institute. https://identitiesjournal.edu.mk/index.php/IJPGC/article/view/413

Lampe, J. R. (2000). *Yugoslavia as history: Twice there was a country*. Cambridge University Press.

Maldini, P., & Pauković, D. (Eds.). (2015). *Croatia and the European Union: Changes and development*. Routledge.

Markovina, D. (2015). *Između crvenog i crnog: Split i Mostar u kulturi sjećanja* [Between red and black: Split and Mostar in the culture of memory]. Algoritam.

Marku, A., & Teqja, E. A. (2024). The European integration process of Western Balkans: Time for a new approach. *Journal of Educational and Social Research, 14*.

Öztürk, A. E. (2021). *Religion, identity and power: Turkey and the Balkans in the twenty-first century*. Edinburgh University Press.

Pavlowitch, S. K. (1999). *A history of the Balkans, 1804–1945*. Longman.

Petrevska, M. (2009). Sam svoj čirak i kalfa i majstor. *Life Magazine*. ISSN 1857-5005.

Prifti, P. R. (1978). *Socialist Albania since 1944: Domestic and foreign developments*. MIT Press.

Roudometof, V. (2001). *Nationalism, globalization, and orthodoxy: The social origins of ethnic conflict in the Balkans*. Greenwood Press.

Said, E. W. (1978). *Orientalism*. Pantheon Books.

Štiks, I. (2015). *Nations and citizens in Yugoslavia and the post-Yugoslav states: One hundred years of citizenship*. Bloomsbury Academic.

Stojanović, D. (2010). *Ulje na vodi: Ogledi iz istorije sadašnjosti*. Peščanik.
Subotić, J. (2011). Europe is a state of mind: Identity and Europeanization in the Balkans. *International Studies Quarterly*, *55*(2), 309–330. https://doi.org/10.1111/j.1468-2478.2011.00649.x
Sugar, P. F. (1977). *Southeastern Europe under Ottoman rule, 1354–1804*. University of Washington Press.
Todorova, M. (1997). *Imagining the Balkans*. Oxford University Press.
Todorova, M. (2009). *Imagining the Balkans* (2nd ed.). Oxford University Press.
Verdery, K. (1996). *What was socialism, and what comes next?* Princeton University Press.
Zimmermann, T., & Jakir, A. (Eds.). (2015). *Europe and the Balkans: Decades of "Europeanization"?* Königshausen & Neumann.
Žižek, S., & Horvat, S. (2014). *What does Europe want? The union and its discontents*. Columbia University Press.

1 Cultural Policy in the Western Balkans

Understanding the Term Cultural Policy

The "Cultural Policy" term is always a challenging task to define, as it combines the two very complex concepts, such as "Culture" on one side, and "Policy" on the other. Palonen (2003) defines policy as a structuring mechanism of political action, essential for regulating activities, standardising practices, and delineating inclusion and exclusion within governance. This aligns with Foucault's (2002a, 2002b) concept of governmentality, which frames governance as a complex multi-actor process involving diverse institutions and tools to shape the power relations. On the other side, the complexity of "culture" as a term is widely recognised in the academic discourse. Acknowledging culture as a structured and dynamic system enriches our reading of the meaning, influence, and importance of cultural policy. The term "culture" has been widely debated and remains one of the most multifaceted concepts in academic discourse. Williams (1976) identified it as one of the most complex words in English, encompassing meanings that range from high art and elite artistic expressions (Garnett & Arnold, 2006, referencing Culture and Anarchy (1869), to Tylor's (1871) foundational anthropological view of culture as a "complex whole" of knowledge, beliefs, and norms. Later scholars, including Boaz (2013), Williams (1981), and Hall (1997) further broadened the concept to emphasise cultural diversity, lived experiences, and the interplay of representation, identity, production, and consumption.

Numerous scholars have attempted to define the term cultural policy, and what is particularly important in these definitions are the political, social, and economic discourses that contextualise these efforts, as well as the historical perspectives from which they emerge. In these academic attempts, the dominant discourses are the western, mostly European, concepts, models, and approaches. This predominant focus of Western cultural policy frameworks often aligns with the economic and intrinsic value of arts and culture, characteristic of neoliberal thought (Holden, 2004, 2006; Klamer, 2017). This orientation tends to dominate over diverse global perspectives, particularly those emanating from Asia, Africa, and other regions, where the cultural policies are often integrated

DOI: 10.4324/9781032724669-2

within community values and collective well-being. For instance, in various Asian nations, as well as in the Western Balkans, cultural policy's focus extends beyond mere economic utility to encompass social cohesion and communal identity, as well as cultural heritage. These policies underscore the intrinsic value of culture as a communal resource rather than a mere commercial asset. In many African countries, cultural policy is also closely linked to attempts to bring back and strengthen traditions that were pushed to the side or completely lost during colonial times. Such policies are frequently designed to amplify local voices and support the rich fabric of cultural expressions found within diverse ethnic communities. The focus here leans towards safeguarding cultural rights, identities, and promoting heritage and diversity, in clear contrast to the market-oriented policies prevalent in Western contexts (Appadurai, 1996; Sen, 2007; Dabashi, 2015; Saad, 2020). However, in the last decades, the emergence of economic superpowers such as China and then western influence in its neoliberal context are reshaping the cultural policy framework in these regions as well, with the predominant discourse of creative and cultural industries seen as a driving force in growing economies (United Nations Development Programme, n.d.).

Since its definition by the United Nations Educational, Scientific and Cultural Organization (UNESCO) in 1969, "cultural policy" has been understood as a comprehensive framework comprising operational principles, administrative practices, and budgetary procedures that guide cultural action by states. These supranational organisations continue to be the key in fostering cultural diversity and democratic empowerment globally on one hand and advancing the creative economy on the other. However, this framework recognises that a universal cultural policy is impractical, as each country tailors its cultural policies to align with its specific political, economic, and social context with different values, goals, and choices.

Cultural policy has continually evolved alongside shifts in societal values, political ideologies, and economic systems, demanding more dynamic and interconnected governance today. In light of contemporary challenges, such as digitalisation, environmental crises, migration, demographic shifts, economic instability, and geopolitical changes, policymakers need to rethink cultural policy frameworks with a foundation in research, radical inclusivity, and adaptability to ensure resilience and relevance.

Cultural Policy in the Western Balkans (WWII – 2024)

The Western Balkans is a political construct and includes the countries of the former Yugoslavia (Bosnia and Herzegovina, Kosovo, Montenegro, North Macedonia, and Serbia) and Albania. After WWII, former Yugoslavia moved to a model of federal multiculturalism and socialism, and at the same time, Albania struggled under Enver Hoxha's regime, leading to complete isolation both internally and externally.

Since the 1990s, the region has been notably affected by the conflict in former Yugoslavia, which had severe negative impacts, characterised with the rise of nationalism, xenophobia, and violence. This period also saw Albania's political opening and the fall of Enver Hoxha's regime.

Despite geographical proximity, former Yugoslavia and Albania underwent very different political, economic, and social transformations, with distinct governance structures and minimal interaction. Therefore, it is crucial to consider these differences when addressing cultural policies for the region. As a result, the cultural policy framework of the Western Balkans is presented separately for each context, including a brief summary of cultural policy in Yugoslavia (1918–1992), the transitional period in 1990s and the current situation in Bosnia and Herzegovina, Kosovo, Montenegro, North Macedonia, and Serbia, as well as the general overview of the Albanian cultural policy discourse during this period.

Cultural Policy in Yugoslavia (WWII – 1992)

The cultural policy of former Yugoslavia, as detailed in Stevan Majstorović's "Cultural Policy in Yugoslavia," published by UNESCO (Majstorović, 1972), represents a distinctive approach that combined decentralisation, autonomy, and unity within a federal socialist framework. This policy acknowledged the country's significant cultural, religious, and linguistic diversity, which greatly influenced its decision-making. At the same time, it aimed to build a unique Yugoslav identity based on the ideology of "Bratstvo Jedinstvo" ("Brotherhood and Unity") under strong central government control. It sought to promote a collective Yugoslav identity by emphasising ethnic harmony and solidarity among the diverse nationalities within the federation (Djokić, 2003; Ramet, 2006). Under the leadership of the Communist Party and strong central government control, this concept aimed to suppress nationalist tensions and foster loyalty to the unified socialist state (Banac, 1984). While "Bratstvo Jedinstvo" served as an official narrative of unity and equality, it often masked underlying ethnic divisions and political inequalities that later resurfaced (Ramet, 2006). Each of the six republics (Bosnia and Herzegovina, Croatia, Macedonia, Montenegro, Serbia, and Slovenia) and the two autonomous provinces (Kosovo and Vojvodina, as part of Serbia) within the federation maintained significant autonomy. This allowed cultural development to be tailored to their specific needs, reflecting the diverse historical and cultural backgrounds of the region. However, the cultural policy framework in that time was not that simple. According to Dragićević Šešić and Stojković (2011), the cultural policy model of Yugoslavia after WWII was close to the bureaucratic-emancipatory model, where the decision-makers used the ideological apparatus to strongly influence and make permanent political pressure on the arts and cultural field, conducted by the central (federal) government.

This model of cultural policy that was established in former Yugoslavia significantly differed from the acclaimed Western models.

Yugoslavian cultural policy can be categorised into three distinct phases in this period: the centralistic and state socialist phase (1946–mid-1950s), the transitional phase (mid-1950s–1974), and the self-governing phase (from 1975 onwards, marked by the establishment of republican and municipal self-government units) (Cvjetičanin & Katunarić, 2001; Simjanovska, 2011).

The period after 1945 marked the beginning of extensive government intervention in culture. This included the establishment of basic institutions, strengthening human resource capacities, democratising and popularising culture and art, and building a new Yugoslav identity. In this period, the first cultural institutions were created, which are crucial for the contemporary history of Yugoslavian culture (Doknić et al., 2009). During this time, the first strategic cultural plan was formulated, in line with the first Five-Year Plan (1947–1951), aiming to enhance cultural infrastructure, including the initiation of domestic film production (PA, 1948). According to Makuljević, a central aspect of this period was the reconsideration of artistic ideology and its role in constructing and accepting Socialist Realism (Makuljević, n.d.).

A significant shifting point in this cultural policy happened during the Writers' Congress in Ljubljana in 1952, when the division from the Soviet Union was publicly announced. There, Miroslav Krleža, one of the leading Croatian writers of the time, gave an important speech, where he criticised Soviet Socialist Realism, particularly in visual art, considering it a regressive move that adopted obsolete bourgeois academic forms (Krležijana, 1993–1999).

In the same period, Modernist expression became a defining feature of Yugoslav artistic practice, playing a significant role in both the artistic landscape and foreign policy. This movement emphasised innovation and a break from traditional forms, which resonated with Yugoslavia's desire to carve out a unique identity distinct from the Soviet influence. Through participation in various international exhibitions, Yugoslav modern art gained prominence, showcasing the country's cultural uniqueness within the socialist bloc while rejecting the constraints of Soviet Socialist Realism. This strategic cultural positioning also helped Yugoslavia align itself with a wide array of culturally diverse nations, emphasising its openness and progressive outlook. The impact of Yugoslav modern art continues to be recognised today. In 2018, the Museum of Modern Art in New York organised an exhibition "Towards a Concrete Utopia: Architecture in Yugoslavia, 1948–1980" dedicated to Yugoslav modern art, which was highly accepted and celebrated by the audience (The Museum of Modern Art, n.d.). The New Yorker praised this particular exhibition, highlighting its importance in understanding the broader narrative of modern art and Yugoslavia's influential role within it (McGuirk, 2018).

From 1951 to the mid-1970s, the Yugoslav government began to actively intervene in cultural affairs, focusing on creating a network of cultural institutions and promoting the democratisation and popularisation of culture and the arts. Influenced by the French cultural policy model of democratisation, Yugoslavia's post-war cultural policy invested heavily in the development of cultural infrastructure (Simjanovska, 2011). A key manifestation of this policy was the construction of numerous Houses of Culture (Domovi na kultura), alongside libraries, museums, and concert halls across the country. These institutions served not only as venues for artistic performances and exhibitions but also as vital spaces for political education, community gathering, and promotion of socialist values (Luthar & Pušnik, 2010). The Houses of Culture were intended to make culture accessible to broader segments of the population, bringing urban and rural divides together. Even small towns and villages with populations of 30,000 or less had Houses of Culture with auditoriums seating up to 1,500 people, although these were often underutilised due to the limited local audience. Despite the underuse, the construction of these cultural centres was driven by the ideology of fostering national cultural exchange, promoting national arts, and educating and entertaining the public. However, the Houses of Culture often remained underused, and their maintenance became very expensive.

The move towards self-governance in 1974, mirroring the broader political and economic model of self-governing socialism, marked a significant shift (Đukić, 2010). Despite the emphasis on autonomy and pluralism, cultural policy in Yugoslavia remained subject to ideological influences and shifts. The state continued to promote the principles of socialist realism, although with certain flexibility and tolerance for alternative artistic expressions. Cultural institutions and cultural events, according to Karaulić (2023), were expected to contribute to the promotion of socialist values and the building of a cohesive Yugoslav identity, while also reflecting the cultural diversity of the country.

Cultural education was integrated into the public education system, focused mainly on arts and cultural production and cultural heritage. The Academies of Sciences and Arts, in each republic of Yugoslavia, were gradually becoming the proponents of national culture. Moreover, reflecting Yugoslavia's non-aligned status during the Cold War, openness to international influences enriched the cultural landscape and showcased Yugoslav culture globally (Bennett, 2011).

This framework effectively managed the nation's cultural policy for a certain period. However, in 1980, after the death of the president Josip Broz Tito, the Federal structure began to reveal weaknesses, and differing opinions on important issues emerged (Jović, 2009; Ramet, 2006). In the 1990s, this system faced significant challenges as rising nationalism, economic crises, external influences, and other destabilising factors led to a conflict with profound negative impacts, both within Yugoslavia and across the broader region. The rise of nationalism not only undermined the previously established cohesive cultural framework but also intensified tensions that extended beyond the nation's borders, significantly affecting regional peace and stability in the long run (Ramet, 2006; Bieber, 2006).

After the fall of Yugoslavia, new independent countries emerged.

The Transitional Model of Cultural Policy in Bosnia and Herzegovina, Kosovo, Montenegro, North Macedonia, Serbia (1990–2024)

Following the dissolution of Yugoslavia in the early 1990s, several successor states pursued independent trajectories of political and economic development. Slovenia and Croatia successfully transitioned earlier and became members of the European Union – Slovenia in 2004 and Croatia in 2013 (Štiks, 2015; Bieber, 2018). The remaining former Yugoslav republics, Bosnia and Herzegovina, Montenegro, North Macedonia, and Serbia, along with Kosovo, which was formerly an autonomous province within Serbia and declared independence in 2008 (a status still disputed by Serbia and not universally recognized), gradually became identified with the political construct known as the "Western Balkans." These countries underwent distinctive yet interconnected transitional processes, often characterised by delayed sovereignty, contested state-building, and complex political transformations. After achieving varying degrees of international recognition, particularly through accession to the United Nations, these states broadly moved towards the adoption of democratic governance and market-oriented reforms. However, the pathways of transition were neither uniform nor linear; they were frequently marked by political instability, hybrid regimes, and unresolved sovereignty issues (Bieber, 2018). The cases of Serbia, Montenegro, and Kosovo exemplify particularly complex and contested developments, shaped by internal conflicts, and prolonged processes of institutional consolidation. Therefore, this analysis focuses specifically on the Western Balkans, where transitional challenges have been most profound and continue to shape the region's political, social, and cultural dynamics.

Dragićević Šešić and Dragojević (2005) argue that the cultural sector faced instability due to crises in public policies, lack of coordination and inadequate communication between the governments (public), private, and independent (civil) sectors, and a crisis in institutional structure. In addition, this region lacks explicit cultural policies and instruments, insufficient sustainable funding and support, unstable political environments, politicisation, corruption, marginalisation of minority groups, limited organisational capacity building, underdeveloped markets, insufficient professional human resources, inadequate competencies to align with EU integration processes, and lack of support for regional and international cooperation (Simjanovska, 2013; Brkić, 2012; Đukić-Dojčinović, 2003).

During this transitional period, the creation of new narratives in identity formation coincided with efforts for accession into the EU. The aspiration for this membership remains a crucial foundation for these countries' fragile democracies and stability. However, the accession process has numerous obstacles, including unresolved disputes with neighbouring countries (such as between Kosovo and Serbia, and North Macedonia and Bulgaria), the complex situation in Bosnia and Herzegovina, increasing scepticism within the EU about further enlargement, and rising Euroscepticism in the Western Balkans.

Analysis of the European Commission's Reports on these countries' integration processes reveals significant and similar challenges. Despite long-standing advocacy, reforms in education, justice, culture, health, and administration remain incomplete. The process of democratisation of the societies is slow, and consequently, growth of the civil sector is slow. In addition, the integration process is currently a struggle between pro-European reformers and populist ethno-nationalist autocrats (European Commission, Directorate-General for Neighbourhood and Enlargement Negotiations, 2023a, 2023b, 2023c, 2023d, 2023e, 2023f; European Commission, 2021, 2023b).

In the context of major social, economic, and political changes, these different challenges show the difficulties in both preserving and changing cultural systems. All Western Balkans countries continue to navigate a complex path towards EU integration, obstructed by internal and external challenges, which directly and indirectly affect the cultural policy framework.

Actors in Change: Civil Society's Influence on Cultural Policy Development in the Western Balkans

In the transitional period of the Western Balkans, civil society actors emerged as crucial forces in shaping democratic processes and cultural policy frameworks. While Slovenia and Croatia quickly integrated into European structures, the remaining countries, including Bosnia and Herzegovina, Kosovo, Montenegro, North Macedonia, and Serbia, faced more prolonged and contested transformations, with cultural development becoming one of the critical battlegrounds for democratic consolidation.

Across the region, the civil society sector grew rapidly during the late 1990s and early 2000s, positioning itself as a dynamic driver of social change. These cultural independent organisations played multifaceted roles: supervising democratic processes, reviving community responsibilities, helping in conflict resolution, creating a sense of belonging, represent the countries internationally, and providing platforms for public dialogue (Simjanovska, 2011). Artists, intellectuals, and independent activists were among the first to push for open dialogue and intercultural exchange, challenging the dominance of state-centred narratives. Despite these efforts, governments across the Western Balkans often viewed independent cultural initiatives with suspicion, leading to the marginalisation of civil society actors rather than their institutional support.

The cultural independent sector, despite these obstacles, developed strong organisational capacities. This sector employed highly educated personnel, demonstrated high degrees of professionalism, championed human rights, promoted intercultural competencies, engaged in international networking, and introduced innovative practices even with limited resources (Simjanovska, 2011). They became critical agents of knowledge transfer, community mobilisation, and creative innovation in the cultural field. However, significant structural weaknesses persisted: an overreliance on foreign donors, underdeveloped models of cultural entrepreneurship, insufficient cooperation with the private sector, and fragile partnerships among civil organisations themselves.

These patterns reflect broader systemic challenges that characterise the cultural sectors throughout the Western Balkans. Independent cultural scenes, although serving as key drivers of artistic innovation, remain fragile and often sidelined by official institutions (Milevska, 2009; Tanurovska-Kjulavkovski, 2018). Research shows that cultural professionals continue to operate under precarious conditions, facing unstable funding opportunities, limited institutional recognition, and policy marginalisation (Cvetičanin, 2011; Cvetičanin & Birešev, 2012; Cvetičanin et al., 2023). Dragićević Šešić and Dragojević (2005) highlight that strategic cultural policy frameworks remain fragmented, further impeding sustainable development. Participation in cultural activities remains low and unequally distributed, mirroring broader social and economic inequalities (Tomka, 2016).

Civil society organisations have played, and continue to play, a crucial role in advocating for cultural diversity as a key component of sustainable development. Building on these efforts, the late twentieth century saw the emergence of participatory approaches and audience engagement strategies that further democratised cultural policy, emphasising the active involvement of communities and individuals in the processes of cultural creation, distribution, consumption, and decision-making (Vidović & Žuvela, 2018). These developments aimed to promote more inclusive, representative, and dynamic cultural landscapes across the Western Balkans.

In sum, civil society organisations have been indispensable in promoting cultural democratisation and innovation across the Western Balkans. However, their work continues to be shaped by precarious structures, external funding dependencies, and limited policy support. Despite these challenges, civil society remains a vital actor in navigating the cultural and democratic transitions of the region.

Recent Developments in Western Balkans' Cultural Policy Framework

Bosnia and Herzegovina

The war in Bosnia and Herzegovina was stopped by signing the General Framework Agreement for Peace in 1995, also known as the Dayton Agreement (United Nations, 1995). With this framework, the constitutional structure and authorities were framed in the Federation of Bosnia and Herzegovina and Republika Srpska and District Brchko, as entities and in addition in cantons and municipalities. All these entities separately regulate the cultural policy framework, having separate ministries of culture characterised by significant differences. According to Kalender (2014), although a federal Ministry of Culture and Sports exists in the Federation of Bosnia and Herzegovina, the principal authority over cultural matters lies with the ten cantons. Each canton typically manages its own Ministry of Culture, often combined with departments for education, science, and sports. Recognised as the most significant cultural hub in the country, the Sarajevo Canton uniquely has a distinct Ministry of Culture and Sport. It has the largest cultural budget in Bosnia and Herzegovina, a highly functional cultural management system, and a relatively well-defined legislative framework for CCI. To sum up, the federal ministry primarily serves a coordinating role among the cantonal ministries, but it lacks substantial authority and is financially and institutionally weakened. Thus, the cantonal governments are the primary actors and bear full responsibility for cultural governance within the Federation.

According to the same author, Kalender (2014), the Republika Srpska entity has a centralised system where the Ministry of Education and Culture, through its Sub-Department of Culture, holds comprehensive powers over cultural affairs. Local governments address cultural needs according to the law. Furthermore, the Brchko District, which was established as an autonomous entity in 2000, has its own cultural governance structure under the Department for Economic Development, Sports, and Culture.

Considering this complicated structure, Bosnia and Herzegovina's cultural governance is highly fragmented, with a decentralised approach in the Federation, a centralised model in RS, and a separate administration in Brchko District. This complexity, involving 14 different ministries, poses significant challenges for systematic cultural development and long-term sustainability.

This structure has resulted in significant fragmentation and neglect of national cultural institutions, which suffer from inadequate financial support and political ignorance. In its rich multicultural heritage, characterised by a diverse population including Muslims, Orthodox Christians, Catholics, Jews, and Roma, the cultural field is facing challenges in being not adequately supported by the existing cultural policies and structures (United Nations Development Programme [UNDP] Bosnia and Herzegovina, 2008).

The cultural policy framework in Bosnia and Herzegovina is manifested through a series of key strategic documents that outline the country's approach to cultural development, diversity, heritage preservation, and CCI. The Development Strategy of the Federation of Bosnia and Herzegovina 2010–2020 (Vlada Federacije BiH, 2020) was a key document for promoting creative initiatives, cultural diversity, intercultural dialogue, social cohesion, protecting art, preserving and protecting heritage, cultural tourism, and embracing the digital transformation of the CCI sector. Likewise, the Cultural Development Strategy of Republika Srpska 2010–2015 (Vlada Republike Srpske, 2010) aims to enhance Republika Srpska's ability to grow its cultural industries (Havoli et al., 2023).

The latest strategy for the Federation of Bosnia and Herzegovina (2021–2027) lacks specific measures or tools dedicated to culture. Instead, it addresses culture indirectly through initiatives aimed at promoting digitalisation across society and strengthening both the public and private sectors (Vlada Federacije Bosne i Hercegovine, 2020).

The current cultural policy framework emphasises national identity and politics over cultural integration and modernisation, neglecting the role of culture in fostering societal dialogue and reconciliation. Creative industries are recognised as a potential of the country; however, no explicit instruments for the development of this sector have been planned at the national level (Bosna i Hercegovina Vijeće Ministara Direkcija za Ekonomsko Planiranje, 2015). Only several local attempts and strategies for development of CCI occurred, such as their Strategy for CCI development of the Sarajevo Canton (Institute for Development Planning of Sarajevo Canton, 2021).

Bakić (2022), in the policy paper, argues that for Bosnia and Herzegovina to achieve sustainable societal development, cultural policy must be integrated with education, economic, and social policies, engaging all concerned stakeholders in the cultural ecosystem. Promoting cultural diversity, fostering intercultural dialogue, and encouraging citizen participation are identified as key components for unifying society. The policy paper also highlights the importance of bringing culture closer to rural and smaller towns to prevent marginalisation and exclusion, promoting broader access to cultural activities, and fostering cultural democratisation and social integration (Bakić, 2022).

In conclusion, the cultural policy framework in Bosnia and Herzegovina needs significant reform to address its fragmented state and structures, develop the potential of CCI, and at the same time address clearly the importance of culture as a tool for societal cohesion.

Kosovo

Following the 1999 conflict in Kosovo, the United Nations has led international efforts to administer and stabilise the region and has issued Resolution 1244, (United Nations Security Council, 1999), from which the United

Nations Interim Administration Mission in Kosovo (UNMIK) was established. This mission was designed to provide temporary governance in Kosovo, allowing its people substantial self-rule. UNMIK was tasked with comprehensive responsibilities, including complete authority over the territory's legislative, executive, and judicial functions.

However, the situation between Serbia and Kosovo is still not officially resolved. Serbian official authorities persistently view Kosovo as part of Serbia, and on the other, the Albanian population in Kosovo strongly rejects any form of Serbian governance. This deep-seated division complicates the path to a clear and accepted status for Kosovo. The challenge further illuminates the ambivalence of both Serbs and Albanians towards political processes such as municipal elections in Kosovo and general elections in Serbia, underscoring a shared prioritisation of independence over electoral participation. This apathy towards governance frameworks underscores the prevailing quest for autonomy that goes beyond the ethnic lines.

Although Kosovo declared independence on 17 February 2008, and subsequently adopted a new constitution on 15 June 2008, and UNMIK's responsibilities shifted, the international recognition of Kosovo is slow, due to unsolved issues with Serbia (United Nations Peacekeeping, n.d.).

In the period 1999–2008, the cultural challenges in Kosovo were increased by the limitations faced by the United Nations Mission in Kosovo (UNMIK's) Cultural Department, which has been criticised for its lack of resources and absence of a unified cultural policy. This gap makes it harder to protect and promote the diverse cultural heritage of both Serbian and Albanian legacies. Despite isolated initiatives in arts and heritage conservation funded by international foundations, there was a lack of a cohesive strategy or policy direction from UNMIK, indicating a possible preference towards Albanian heritage.

Efforts by the Council of Europe, starting in 2000, to assess and formulate a heritage policy in Kosovo signify a positive shift towards international cooperation and strategic planning. The Council's actions include surveys and pilot projects aimed at the reconstruction and rehabilitation of Kosovo's built heritage.

In response, the National Cultural Heritage Strategy 2017–2027 was developed, aiming to create long-term frameworks that define a clear vision and offer sustainability-based solutions. The strategy focuses on strengthening the infrastructure for safeguarding Kosovo's cultural heritage in terms of legal frameworks, values, and standards. Additionally, it emphasises the importance of fostering sustainable development across economic, social, and cultural sectors.

Despite numerous challenges in this domain, the continuous efforts of the Ministry of Culture, Youth, and Sports (MCYS) and the relevant institutions have prioritised cultural heritage as a key governmental concern (Ministry of Culture, Youth and Sport, 2017).

The new proposed cultural policy in Kosovo (2024), as detailed in the draft Law on Art and Culture, represents a significant legislative reform aiming to modernise and streamline the governance of cultural institutions (Koha Ditore, 2024). This new framework advocates a serious reform in the cultural sector in Kosovo, introducing a new hierarchical structure within cultural institutions, where the traditional roles of artistic leaders will be replaced by directors, who will be selected through a more centralised process involving a public competition and final appointment by the Minister of Culture. Moreover, the management councils currently in place will be dissolved, and professional advisory bodies will be established to assist directors in designing and implementing artistic programmes.

Another important element of the new policy is the establishment of the National Council of Arts, which will serve as an advisory, supervisory, and selection body for the directors of public cultural institutions. Furthermore, the draft law recognises the importance of the independent cultural scene by establishing a Council for the Independent Cultural Scene, which will be responsible for developing long-term policies and strategies for its support through public funding.

This ambitious cultural policy framework by the Kosovar government, led by the Minister of Culture, Hajrulla Çeku, aims to reduce bureaucracy, foster greater artistic freedom, and enhance the financial sustainability of cultural institutions, ultimately contributing to economic growth and social development within Kosovo.

Overall, although the situation with the cultural field and formation of new cultural policy in Kosovo is complex and requires a careful and varied approach from both local leaders and international groups, the current situation is promising and has perspective based on a new energy and force coming from the leading persons in culture in the country.

Montenegro

After the fall of Yugoslavia, Montenegro was part of the Serbia & Montenegro federation, and in 2006, it declared its independence (Britannica, n.d.). Montenegro was part of a larger cultural system primarily oriented towards a socialist cultural model, during which most major cultural institutions were established. After the formation of the Ministry of Culture in 2006, the greatest challenge for the overall cultural system was to establish a new operational definition of national culture.

The modernisation of Montenegro's cultural sector commenced in 2008 with the passage of the Law on Culture, marking a significant shift as outlined in the Compendium for Cultural Policies (Kraljević, 2022). Between 2008 and 2020, the Ministry of Culture implemented various strategies and laws aimed at fostering sustainable and creative pre-conditions for the cultural scene. In this period, more precisely, in 2016, the Ministry of Sustainable Development and Tourism (2016) proposed a substantial tool for the achievement of the UN 2030 Agenda. The document clearly articulates the position of cultural policy, presenting key strategic objectives related to the cultural field: recognise the role and value of arts and culture that can influence a country's economic and social growth, and also develop an efficient and sustainable cultural heritage framework with specific targets set for achievement by 2030.

However, the Montenegrin cultural landscape experienced substantial shifts following the political changes in 2020, when the long-standing ruling party lost its parliamentary majority after three decades. This led to the temporary integration of the Ministry of Culture into the Ministry of Education, Science, Culture, and Sport, a move that faced considerable criticism. By mid-2022, following another political shift, the Ministry of Culture and Media was reinstated. These political and structural changes, coupled with the global post-pandemic context, have extended additional pressure on Montenegro's cultural sector, delaying its progress.

In response, a new national programme for culture emerged in 2023 (2023–2027), setting priorities for the coming years. These priorities include sector development, international collaboration, strengthening diversity, protecting cultural heritage, linking culture with tourism, and developing the potential of the CCI (Ministry of Culture and Media of Montenegro, 2023). In addition, the Institute for Entrepreneurship and Economic Development (IPER) has issued a proposal for development of the Creative Industries in Montenegro in 2019, which are detailed in the next chapter of this book (Institut za preduzetništvo i ekonomski razvoj, 2020).

In conclusion, Montenegro's cultural sector has undergone significant structural transformations, and the introduction of the new national programme for culture in 2023 reflects the ongoing efforts to prioritise cultural development, international collaboration, and heritage protection. Nevertheless, the insufficient focus on the CCI within this programme highlights a gap that needs to be fully addressed (Ministry of Culture and Media of Montenegro, 2023).

North Macedonia

After proclaiming independence and sovereignty in 1991, the Republic of Macedonia shifted from the decentralised cultural framework inherited from the former Yugoslav system to a more centralised structure for its cultural institutions and organisations. The decade between 1991 and 2001, and in some respects continuing to the present day, was marked by the lack of a coherent cultural policy or a scientifically grounded, expert-led long-term vision for cultural development. This period was characterised by intense centralisation, unclear divisions of responsibility, and a reliance on outdated bureaucratic mechanisms of institutional financing, which prioritised rigid, traditional funding schemes over innovative and adaptive cultural strategies.

In 2001, the political and cultural landscape of Macedonia was significantly disrupted by an armed conflict between the Macedonian and Albanian ethnic communities, marking a challenging moment in the nation's recent history. This conflict was resolved through the adoption of the Ohrid Framework Agreement in 2001 (Ministry of Local Self-Government, 2001). The agreement instigated several constitutional amendments, redefining the state from being solely of the Macedonian people to one that also encompasses citizens from various ethnic backgrounds, including Albanian, Turkish, Vlach, Serbian, Roma, Bosniak, and others. Legislative changes were introduced regarding the use of national symbols, and the Badinter principle was implemented to ensure equitable decision-making processes. In addition, the principle of fair representation was established to provide equal employment opportunities for different ethnic groups within the administration. The agreement stated that "any language spoken by at least 20% of the population" would be recognised as an official language, with measures in place for its use in official proceedings and personal documents (Ministry of Local Self-Government, 2001).

In 2007, Macedonia experienced a significant cultural shift when the right-wing, demo-Christian government launched the Skopje 2014 project through the Ministry of Culture. This initiative, described as a transformative force in the nation's political, economic, social, and cultural spheres (Mojanchevska, 2011), involved constructing nearly 20 new buildings and numerous bronze and marble statues, including a triumphal arch and an obelisk. Analysts criticised the project as a form of "social engineering," aiming to build a new nationalistic identity. The project revealed ideological intentions to reshape both the city's and the nation's identity, reflecting frustrations with geopolitical challenges, such as the dispute with Greece over Macedonia's name and issues with neighbouring countries regarding language and religious recognition. The implementation lacked transparency and bordered on questionable legality (Simjanovska, 2013).

During this period, the Macedonian cultural policy, though not explicitly stated, reveals a shift towards a nationalistic monument-building agenda. This approach reflects the deep connection between monuments and the culture of memory, viewing them as essential pillars in the formation of national identity. This framework is characterised as not open and claustrophobic, where the citizens were neglected in the decision-making processes, especially when symbols and monuments were concerned. This approach is the opposite of what Milena Dragićević Šešić (2011a, p. 44) envisions for these societies. She calls for memory and monument policies that unite rather than divide, building bridges between communities, and fostering intercultural dialogue and harmony.

According to the 2022 Cultural Policy Review of the Republic of Macedonia, the country faces significant challenges in shaping a cohesive cultural policy (Kern, 2020). In addition, limited budget resources negatively affect the developmental aspect of the cultural field. However, no explicit policy has yet been formulated to address these sectors. Furthermore, the public administration reform remains a critical issue, with a need for greater transparency, better data collection in cultural sectors, and the digitisation of administrative procedures (Simjanovska, 2022).

Stakeholders have raised concerns over the lack of transparency in funding allocations, which are often delayed and poorly managed. Intellectual property protection, especially with regards to copyright laws, lagging behind EU standards, presents a further challenge for the country's cultural alignment with Europe. Furthermore, the implementation of the national cultural development strategy has been slow, with delays in adopting necessary legislation (Simjanovska, 2022). There are also gaps in education and skills, particularly in getting young people ready for careers in the creative and cultural industry sector.

To sum up, although there is always a political will, at least on a declarative level, for reforms in the cultural sector in North Macedonia, it has yet to be materialised.

Serbia

Serbia's cultural policy has evolved dramatically since 1990, mirroring the country's substantial political, economic, and social transformation. During the 1990s, Serbia was deeply affected by the disintegration of Yugoslavia, wars in the Balkans, and economic sanctions, all of which resulted in the country's isolation from European and global cultural networks. Under the regime of Slobodan Milošević, the state imposed heavy control over cultural production; much of the cultural policy of the time was nationalistic, which focused on preserving a narrow sense of national identity. Cultural institutions were severely underfunded, and the arts sector struggled with lack of resources, although independent artists and cultural movements persisted despite these challenges.

Moreover, this period is characterised by a complex and evolving landscape shaped by the nation's turbulent history, which has witnessed periods of authoritarian rule, economic instability, and significant social change (Dragićević-Šešić et al., 2011). Following the downfall of the Milosević regime in 2000, Serbia has undergone a gradual transformation towards establishing a more democratic and decentralised cultural framework. This shifting point reflects a broader effort to integrate Serbian culture into European and global contexts while fostering a vibrant domestic cultural scene. Cultural policy is aimed at democratisation and decentralisation of cultural institutions, highlighting increased support for the arts and encouraging the development of the independent sector. Initiatives such as participation in European cultural programmes like Culture 2000 and later Creative Europe were part of this effort to re-engage with the broader European cultural sphere. This period was also marked by renewed efforts to align Serbia's cultural policies with European standards, emphasising cultural diversity, heritage preservation, and support for contemporary cultural production.

Another important historic point of the Serbian Cultural Policy was the Belgrade Agreement (2002), when the Federal State of Serbia-Montenegro was established, comprising two distinct republics – Serbia and Montenegro – each maintaining its own culture ministry. Serbia informally included the autonomous provinces of Vojvodina and Kosovo, with the latter under the United Nations administration, hence outside Serbian legal jurisdiction. Vojvodina possessed its own Secretariat for Education and Culture. The relevance of the Belgrade Agreement ended following Montenegro's independence on 21 May 2006, as determined by a referendum. Consequently, Serbia inadvertently also attained independence. In this period, the cultural policy was focused on the reform of key national cultural institutions and the public sector overall, calling for the adoption of innovative management and marketing approaches (Council of the European Union, 2002).

In 2012, Serbia's candidacy for EU membership became a reality, with cultural policy increasingly focused on alignment with European frameworks and fostering the cultural sector's role in economic development (European Commission, n.d.). There were significant investments in cultural infrastructure, including the modernisation of museums and theatres, as well as efforts to promote cultural tourism. Furthermore, digitalisation of cultural heritage emerged as a key priority, reflecting the broader European trends of preserving cultural assets in digital formats. However, funding challenges continued to plague the independent cultural sector, which often struggled to secure adequate resources for its initiatives.

In 2015, the Serbian Cultural Policy, as reported by the Council of Europe, reflects both historical strength and contemporary challenges within the sector. Historically, Serbia has benefitted from a strong tradition of cultural investments, which continues to have a crucial part in its development. Despite political, social, and economic disruptions, particularly following the disintegration of Yugoslavia, Serbia has maintained a substantial cultural infrastructure, including numerous cultural events and institutions that are primarily supported by public funding (Council of Europe, 2015). According to the same report, Serbian cultural policy before 2015 was struggling with modernising this infrastructure to meet contemporary needs. This includes addressing the evolving forms of cultural consumption, internationalising cultural exchanges, and sourcing alternative funding mechanisms, as the public funding levels are challenging to sustain. The policy also emphasises the need for

Serbia to increase its cultural investment to further strengthen and diversify its cultural sector. Challenges identified in this period include reforming and professionalising institutions within the performing arts, balancing support among various cultural and linguistic communities, and revitalising major cultural facilities (Council of Europe, 2015).

The newer Culture Development Strategy of the Republic of Serbia (2020–2029) recognises culture as a crucial element for societal development and international representation (Министарство културе Републике Србије, 2020). Moreover, the strategy focuses on preserving and nurturing Serbia's cultural and historical heritage. It envisions creating a space for free creativity that contributes to the well-being of individuals and society, and meets the cultural needs of its citizens and the Serbian diaspora. The strategy outlines one general goal – improving cultural participation among citizens – as measurable through engagement with cultural institutions and programmes (Министарство културе Републике Србије, 2020). Additionally, it sets specific goals that include regulatory improvements, investment in cultural institutions, development of cultural production and participation, fostering international cooperation and European integration, and advancing digital transformation in the cultural sector. These objectives are designed to strengthen culture as a dynamic component of Serbia's social and institutional framework; however, the strategy does not show clear vision and efforts for developing the CCI.

Despite the comprehensive articulation of the Culture Development Strategy (2020–2029), the current Serbian cultural policy framework is characterised by several critical challenges. Populist tendencies within the ruling party, lack of transparency, and insufficient expertise in decision-making processes hinder effective governance. Furthermore, the marginalisation of civil society, the absence of sound strategic funding mechanisms, and the undervaluation of international collaboration contribute to a discourse that undermines the potential for sustainable cultural development.

From Totalitarianism to Transformation: Cultural Policy in Albania (WWII – 2024)

From 1945 to 1990, Albania was ruled by one of the most repressive regimes, under the dictator Enver Hoxha. The regime was characterised by the refusal of the fundamental human and cultural rights such as freedom of speech, religion, private property, and freedom of movement; by channelling huge amounts of economic resources into unproductive investments, such as building more than 750.000 bunkers in the whole territory of the country; and a complete isolation of the country.

The cultural policy of Albania in this period, manifested in an engineering model, under the dictatorial leadership of Enver Hoxha, adopted a strict, Stalinist-inspired authoritarian approach that was profoundly restrictive, using culture as an instrument for ideological enforcement and political control. According to Stephen R. Bowers, this period was marked by the government's heavy hand, ensuring that all forms of cultural expression conformed strictly to communist ideologies, particularly socialist realism, while vigorously suppressing Western cultural influences (Bowers, 1992). Central to Hoxha's regime was the strategic establishment of cultural institutions meant to reinforce a homogeneous cultural identity that maintained socialist values. These institutions were crucial in promoting state-sponsored art, literature, and performances emphasising the positive aspects of the proletariat, celebrated the achievements of communism, and disseminated party propaganda. Education and literacy campaigns were also manipulated as tools for ideological indoctrination, effectively increasing the literacy rate and extending educational reach across both urban and rural populations, thus deepening the regime's ideological control among the general population.

During this period, the aesthetic of socialist realism prevailed, primarily celebrating the figures of working women and men. According to Berberi and Tummers (2021), the reconstruction of the nation was marked by the building of cultural monuments dedicated to war heroes, alongside significant educational and cultural developments such as the founding of the first University and art education, Galleries, Opera and Ballet. Furthermore, these authors note that in 1967, the regime's proclamation of national atheism led to the prohibition and destruction of religious artefacts, particularly those in public spaces. The introduction of "Albanianism" represented a new ideological framework constructed by the government.

Until 1968, Albania's visual arts and culture closely mirrored those of Russia until the country withdrew from the Warsaw Pact, subsequently aligning more closely with China. This alignment was reflected in showing of Chinese symbols in public domain in Albania, such as Chinese pioneers represented in paintings, posters, films, who stood as representations of the new alliance. During this period, there was a significant growth in the film industry and an increase in the construction of monuments honouring war heroes.

However, artistic freedom was restricted within the limits considered acceptable by the party, often under the direct supervision of its leader, Enver Hoxha. Artworks that did not conform were subject to rejection and destruction, with artists facing severe repercussions such as imprisonment, forced labour, or intensified penalties (Berberi & Tummers, 2021).

Another example of how Hoxha's regime functioned, as pointed out by Bowers, is the literature field that was particularly instrumental, serving as a tool for ideological instruction and social critique. Ismail Kadare (Kadare, 1968), one of Albania's most prominent writers, managed to weave the regime's narratives into his works while also offering subtle critiques of the socio-political order. His novel "The Wedding" illustrates the cultural tension in Albania, depicting the struggle against the country's regressive customs and echoing Hoxha's push for modernisation and secularism. Kadare's literary contributions highlight how Albanian literature during this period was not only a reflection of state policies but also a sophisticated commentary on the complexities of cultural identity and traditional values.

Unfortunately, many creative and free-minded people needed to escape Albania and live in other countries in the Western part of the world, where they can freely express their ideas and critiques towards the regime in Albania. Kadare was one of these, living in France for many years.

The 1990s represented a major turning point in Albania's cultural policy with the fall of Enver Hoxha's regime, replaced with Ramiz Alia, the new leader in Albania. During this time, the economic system started to be re-questioned. In the same period, student protests were generated while the country was going in a deep economic recession. All these shifting points in Albania coincide with the fall of the Berlin Wall. As of then, Albania witnessed and made the first steps towards an open market economy and democracy, under the great and strategic assistance of the international community.

The transition was characterised by a significant opening to global influences, leading to substantial changes in cultural perceptions and management. The Albanian government, free from Hoxha's isolationist policies, began to decentralise cultural management and encouraged a diversity of voices within the cultural sphere.

With no substantial investment in the cultural infrastructure for more than 40 years, and in general in any other field, the country looks pretty grey and depressing. In that very moment, a young artist, although controversial, educated in France, named Edi Rama, appeared in the political scene, and made a huge impact on the cultural landscape. He was a mayor of Tirana, and in his mandate, he, together with several well-known artists, has made a huge intervention in the city of Tirana, painted the buildings in strong and vivid colours, transforming the city into a vivid and open place. As a minister of Culture, and later as a prime minister of the Albanian government (since 2013), he has shown strong political will in developing the cultural field in Albania (Kern, 2018).

This era saw the proliferation of private and civil society cultural institutions, the revival of suppressed religious traditions, and the establishment of media outlets that brought a fresh breath of pluralism to the Albanian cultural landscape.

According to the New strategy for Culture for 2019–2025 (Ministry of Culture of Albania, 2019), Albanian's cultural policy of today is increasingly directed towards pluralism, diversity, innovation, creative industries, international cooperation, balancing globalisation with the preservation of national heritage, linking culture and sport, and connecting with the tourism.

The government is focused on leveraging Albania's cultural diversity as a strength rather than a liability, and also as crucial components of socioeconomic development. This shift represents a mature understanding of culture as a dynamic and integrative force in national and international contexts.

To summarise, the transformation of Albanian cultural policy from the post-WWII era till today consists of a shift from rigid, ideologically driven regimes to a more liberal, inclusive, and diversified approach. This evolution not only highlights the shifting political mindset but also emphasises the intricate relationship between politics and culture in shaping national identity and socioeconomic progress.

References

Appadurai, A. (1996). *Modernity at large: Cultural dimensions of globalization*. University of Minnesota Press.

Arnold, M. (1869). *Culture and anarchy and other selected prose* (P. J. Keating, Ed.). Penguin Classics. (Original work published 1869)

Bakić, S. (2022). *Cultural policy in Bosnia and Herzegovina: Recognising culture as an integration tool (ÖGfE policy brief 16/2022)*. Österreichische Gesellschaft für Europapolitik. https://www.oegfe.at/policy-briefs/cultural-policy-in-bosnia-and-herzegovina/

Banac, I. (1984). *The national question in Yugoslavia: Origins, history, politics*. Cornell University Press.

Bennett, C. (2011). *Yugoslavia's bloody collapse: Causes, course and consequences* (2nd ed.). NYU Press.

Berberi, B., & Tummers, K. (2021). *Country profile: Albania*. Compendium of Cultural Policies and Trends. http://www.culturalpolicies.net

Bieber, F. (2006). *Post-war Bosnia: Ethnicity, inequality and public sector governance*. Palgrave Macmillan.

Bieber, F. (2018). *The rise of authoritarianism in the Western Balkans*. Palgrave Macmillan.

Boaz, D. P. (2013). *Being the whole: Toward the emerging noetic revolution* (Draft). Copper Mountain Institute.

Bosna i Hercegovina Vijeće Ministara Direkcija za Ekonomsko Planiranje. (2015). *Strateški okvir za BiH*. Sarajevo, Bosnia and Herzegovina. http://www.dep.gov.ba

Bowers, S. R. (1992). *Ethnic politics in Eastern Europe*. London: Research Institute for the Study of Conflict and Terrorism.

Britannica. (n.d.). *Montenegro: Independence*. Encyclopædia Britannica. https://www.britannica.com/place/Montenegro/Independence

Brkić, A. (2012). *Cultural policy frameworks: (Re)constructing national and supranational identities: The Balkans and the European Union*. European Cultural Foundation.

Council of Europe. (2015). *Cultural policy peer review of Serbia: Art and culture, an investment for Serbia's future*. https://rm.coe.int

Council of the European Union. (2002). *Agreement on principles of relations between Serbia and Montenegro within the state union.* https://www.consilium.europa.eu

Cvetičanin, P. (2011). Vaninstitucionalni akteri kulturne politike u Srbiji, Crnoj Gori i Makedoniji. *Kultura, 130*, 265–290.

Cvetičanin, P., & Birešev, A. (Eds.). (2012). *Social and cultural capital in Western Balkan societies.* Centre for Empirical Cultural Studies of South-East Europe.

Cvetičanin, P., Nikolić, T., & Bobičić, N. (2023). *Gender and labor in the cultural field in Serbia.* Independent Culture Scene of Serbia; Faculty of Arts, University of Niš.

Cvjetičanin, B., & Katunarić, V. (Eds.). (2001). *Croatia in the 21st century: Strategy of cultural development.* Ministry of Culture of the Republic of Croatia.

Dabashi, H. (2015). *Can non-Europeans think?* Bloomsbury Publishing.

Djokić, D. (2003). *Yugoslavism: Histories of a failed idea, 1918–1992.* C. Hurst & Co.

Doknić, B., Petrović, M. F., & Hofman, I. (Eds.). (2009). *Kulturna politika Jugoslavije: 1945–1952: Zbornik dokumenata.* Arhiv Jugoslavije.

Dragićević Šešić, M. (2011a). Cultural policies, identities and monument building in Southeastern Europe. In A. Milohnić & N. Švob-Đokić (Eds.), *Cultural identity politics in the (post)transitional societies* (pp. 31–46). Institute for International Relations.

Dragićević-Šešić, M., Brkić, A., & Mikić, H. (2011). *Country profile: Serbia.* Compendium of Cultural Policies and Trends in Europe. http://www.culturalpolicies.net

Dragićević Šešić, M., & Dragojević, S. (2005). *Arts management in turbulent times: Adaptable quality management.* Boekmanstudies.

Dragićević Šešić, M., & Stojković, B. (2011). *Kultura: menadžment, animacija, marketing.* CLIO.

Đukić-Dojčinović, V. (2003). *Tranzicione kulturne politike: konfuzije i dileme.* Zadužbina Andrejević.

Đukić, V. (2010). *Država i kultura: Studije savremene kulturne politike.* Beograd: Fakultet dramaskih umetnosti.

European Commission. (2021). *2021 enlargement package.* https://neighbourhood-enlargement.ec.europa.eu

European Commission. (n.d.). *Serbia – enlargement policy.* https://neighbourhood-enlargement.ec.europa.eu

European Commission, Directorate-General for Neighbourhood and Enlargement Negotiations. (2023a). *Albania report 2023.* https://neighbourhood-enlargement.ec.europa.eu

European Commission, Directorate-General for Neighbourhood and Enlargement Negotiations. (2023b). *Bosnia and Herzegovina report 2023.* https://neighbourhood-enlargement.ec.europa.eu

European Commission, Directorate-General for Neighbourhood and Enlargement Negotiations. (2023c). *Kosovo report 2023.* https://neighbourhood-enlargement.ec.europa.eu

European Commission, Directorate-General for Neighbourhood and Enlargement Negotiations. (2023d). *Montenegro report 2023*. https://neighbourhood-enlargement.ec.europa.eu

European Commission, Directorate-General for Neighbourhood and Enlargement Negotiations. (2023e). *North Macedonia report 2023*. https://neighbourhood-enlargement.ec.europa.eu

European Commission, Directorate-General for Neighbourhood and Enlargement Negotiations. (2023f). *Serbia report 2023*. https://neighbourhood-enlargement.ec.europa.eu

Foucault, M. (2002a). Governmentality. In J. D. Faubion (Ed.), *Michel Foucault: Power* (Vol. 3, pp. 201–222). Penguin Books.

Foucault, M. (2002b). Interview with Michel Foucault. In J. D. Faubion (Ed.), *Michel Foucault: Power* (Vol. 3, pp. 239–297). Penguin Books.

Garnett, J., & Arnold, M. (2006). *Culture and anarchy (Oxford world's classics)*. Oxford University Press.

Hall, S. (Ed.). (1997). *Representation: Cultural representations and signifying practices*. SAGE.

Havoli, B., Fairburn, J., Pugh, J., Talam, E., Efendic, A., & Stojcic, N. (2023). *Promoting the creative sector in three deindustrialised economies: The United Kingdom, Bosnia and Herzegovina, and Croatia (project report)*. Staffordshire University.

Holden, J. (2004). *Capturing cultural value*. Demos.

Holden, J. (2006). *Cultural value and the crisis of legitimacy*. Demos.

Institut za preduzetništvo i ekonomski razvoj. (2020). *Smjernice za razvoj kulturnih i kreativnih industrija u Crnoj Gori*. https://kreativneindustrije.me

Institute for Development Planning of Sarajevo Canton. (2021). *Sarajevo Canton development strategy 2021–2027*. https://zpr.ks.gov.ba

Jović, D. (2009). *Yugoslavia: A state that withered away*. West Lafayette, IN: Purdue University Press.

Kadare, I. (1968). *The wedding*. Naim Frasheri Publishing House.

Kalender, A. (2014). Country report: Bosnia and Herzegovina. In V. Simjanovska, V. Ratzenböck, & A. Kalender (Eds.), *Kulturlogue* (pp. 20–34). Performing Arts Center Multimedia.

Karaulić, J. (2023). *Kulturne izvedbe Jugoslovenstva*. Clio.

Kern, P. (2018). *A cultural strategy for Albania: Implanting the cultural bug*. KEA European Affairs; Council of Europe.

Kern, P. (2020). *Cultural policy review of the Republic of North Macedonia: Towards a strategy for heritage and the development of culture and creative industries*. Council of Europe.

Klamer, A. (2017). *Doing the right thing: A value based economy*. Ubiquity Press.

Koha Ditore. (2024). *The government announces the new cultural policy for the dignity of the artist*. https://www.koha.net/en/culture/383518/the-government-announces-the-new-cultural-policy-for-the-dignity-of-the-artist

Kraljević, N. (2022). *Montenegro: Short cultural policy profile 2022*. Compendium of Cultural Policies and Trends. https://www.culturalpolicies.net

Krležijana. (1993–1999). *Govor na Kongresu književnika u Ljubljani*. Leksikografski zavod Miroslav Krleža. https://krlezijana.lzmk.hr

Luthar, B., & Pušnik, M. (Eds.). (2010). *Remembering utopia: The culture of everyday life in socialist Yugoslavia*. New Academia Publishing.

Majstorović, S. (1972). *Cultural policy in Yugoslavia* (Studies and documents on cultural policies). UNESCO.

Makuljević, N. (n.d.). *Yugoslav art and culture: From the art of a nation to the art of a territory*. YU Historija. https://www.yuhistorija.com

McGuirk, J. (2018). The unrepeatable architectural moment of Yugoslavia's "Concrete Utopia". *The New Yorker*. https://www.newyorker.com/culture/culture-desk/the-unrepeatable-architectural-moment-of-yugoslavias-concrete-utopia

Milevska, S. (2009). *Gender Difference in the Balkans: Archives of representations of gender difference and agency in visual culture and contemporary art in the Balkans*. Saarbrücken, Germany: VDM Verlag.

Ministry of Culture and Media of Montenegro. (2023, December 1). *Nacionalni program razvoja kulture 2023–2027*. https://www.gov.me

Ministry of Culture of Albania. (2019). *National strategy for culture 2019–2025*. https://kultura.gov.al

Ministry of Culture, Youth and Sport, Republic of Kosovo. (2017). *National strategy for cultural heritage 2017–2027*. Prishtinë: Ministry of Culture, Youth and Sport of the Republic of Kosovo.

Ministry of Culture, Youth and Sports of the Republic of Kosovo. (2024). *Concept Document on Art and Culture* [Draft policy document]

Ministry of Local Self-Government. (2001, August 13). *Framework agreement*. https://mls.gov.mk

Ministry of Sustainable Development and Tourism, Montenegro. (2016). *National strategy for sustainable development of Montenegro*. https://faolex.fao.org

Mojanchevska, K. (2011). Representation of diversity in the public space of societies in transition: Case study of the city of Skopje. In V. Simjanovska (Ed.), *Re-thinking local cultural policy: New identity and new paradigm* (pp. 73–94). PAC Multimedia.

The Museum of Modern Art. (n.d.). *Toward a concrete utopia: Architecture in Yugoslavia, 1948–1980*. MoMA. https://www.moma.org

PA. (1948). Yugoslavia's five-year plan: The economic background of the cominform split. *The World Today*, *4*(8), 331–336.

Palonen, K. (2003). Four times of politics: Policy, polity, politicking, and politicization. *Alternatives*, *28*(2), 171–186.

Ramet, S. P. (2006). *The Three Yugoslavias: State-building and legitimation, 1918–2005*. Bloomington, IN: Indiana University Press; Washington, DC: Woodrow Wilson Center Press.

Saad, L. F. (2020). *Me and white supremacy: Combat racism, change the world, and become a good ancestor*. Sourcebooks, Inc.

Sen, A. (2007). *Identity and violence: The illusion of destiny*. Penguin Books India.

Simjanovska, V. (2011). *Re-thinking local cultural policy*. PAC Multimedia.

Simjanovska, V. (2013). *Possible new model of cultural policy of the Republic of Macedonia in multicultural context* [PhD thesis, University of Arts in Belgrade].

Simjanovska, V. (2022). *Report on the impact of COVID-19 on the cultural and creative industries (CCIs) in North Macedonia*. Cultural Relations Platform.

Tanurovska–Kjulavkovski, B. (2018). *Theory of institutions and cultural policies for contemporary performative practices* (Doctoral dissertation, Faculty of Dramatic Arts, University of Belgrade).

Tomka, G. (2016). *Audience is watching you: Challenges to audience development by independent cultural organisations in Bosnia and Herzegovina, Macedonia and Serbia*. Youth Cultural Center – Bitola.

Tylor, E. B. (1871). *Primitive culture: Researches into the development of mythology, philosophy, religion, art and custom* (Vol. 2). J. Murray.

United Nations. (1995). *Letter dated 29 November 1995 from the permanent representative of the United States of America to the United Nations addressed to the secretary-general*. https://peacemaker.un.org

United Nations Development Programme. (n.d.). *Accelerating creativity and innovation in Africa*. UNDP Ghana. https://www.undp.org

United Nations Development Programme Bosnia and Herzegovina. (2008). *Revised standard joint programme document: Improving cultural understanding in Bosnia and Herzegovina*. http://www.mdgfund.org

United Nations Peacekeeping. (n.d.). *United Nations interim administration mission in Kosovo (UNMIK)*. https://peacekeeping.un.org

United Nations Security Council. (1999). *Resolution 1244 (1999)*. https://documents.un.org

Vidović, D., & Žuvela, A. (2018). Key terms and concepts for understanding participatory governance in culture. In *Do it together* (pp. 16–45). Biblioteka Kultura Nova.

Vlada Republike Srpske. (2010). *Strategija razvoja kulture Republike Srpske 2010–2015* [Cultural Development Strategy of Republika Srpska 2010–2015]. Banja Luka: Vlada Republike Srpske.

Vlada Federacije Bosne i Hercegovine. (2020). *Strategija razvoja Federacije Bosne i Hercegovine 2021–2027*. https://faolex.fao.org

Williams, R. (1976). *Keywords: A vocabulary of culture and society*. Oxford University Press.

Williams, R. (1981). *Culture*. Fontana.

Министарство културе Републике Србије. (2020). *Стратегија развоја културе Републике Србије од 2020. до 2029*. Министарство културе Републике Србије.

2 Cultural and Creative Industries in the Western Balkans

The Emergence of Cultural and Creative Industries: Global Framing and Regional Relevance

The emergence of CCI is closely tied to the broader socioeconomic transition from industrial to post-industrial societies and the redefinition of culture's societal role. Early critiques by Adorno and Horkheimer (1944, 1979) described the "cultural industry" as a system of mass-produced cultural goods, serving political and economic interests while eroding artistic autonomy and intrinsic value. Although influential, this perspective has been challenged for its one-dimensional understanding of commodification and failure to address the evolving role of technology and market complexity in cultural production (Garnham, 1990; Mège, 1989; Ryan, 1992; Flew, 2012).

The policy recognition of CCI began to solidify in the 1990s, notably with Australia's Creative Nation report (Department of Communications, Information Technology and the Arts, 1994) and the UK's strategic reorientation under the New Labour government. Here, culture was reframed as both a public good and an economic asset, addressing the need to democratise access and justify cultural funding through economic returns (McGuigan, 1996, 2009; Hartley, 2021). This shift also responded to critiques of the existing arts funding system as elitist (Bianchini & Parkinson, 1993). According to Hartley (2021), the concept was driven more by political reform than by economic, cultural, or academic theory, aiming to align cultural governance with entrepreneurial and industrial policies. O'Connor (2010) further notes that this redefinition sought to renegotiate the relationship between the state and the cultural field.

The UK's 1998 Creative Industries Task Force adopted the term "creative industries" to encompass a broader range of sectors based on individual creativity, skill, and intellectual property, formalised in the definition introduced by the Department for Digital, Culture, Media and Sport (1998). This understanding became globally influential and has since shaped national and supranational cultural policy frameworks (Galloway & Dunlop, 2007; Throsby, 2008).

DOI: 10.4324/9781032724669-3

Today, the global economic and social significance of CCI is undeniable. According to the UNESCO (2022) and the United Nations Conference on Trade and Development (2024), the sector contributes 3.1% to global Gross Domestic Product (GDP), generates €2.1 trillion in revenue, and employs around 50 million people – 6.2% of the total global workforce. CCI are increasingly recognised as key drivers of economic growth, innovation, urban regeneration, and international trade (UNESCO, 2022; Howkins, 2001).

However, applying global models to regional contexts such as the Western Balkans poses challenges. As Dragicevic Sesic (n.d.) argues, claims about the creative economy fostering global democratisation overlook the unequal structures that persist in global cultural trade. The assumption of a decentralised, multipolar, and non-hierarchical creative system is more idealistic than reflective of reality. For transitional and post-conflict societies, such as those in the Western Balkans, cultural policies must account for complex socio-political conditions, local traditions, and fragile cultural infrastructures.

In parallel, several emerging concepts have further expanded the discourse around CCI. Terms such as the creative class (Florida, 2002, 2005) and creative economy (Howkins, 2001; Throsby, 2008; United Nations Conference on Trade and Development, 2010; Hartley, 2021) have sought to capture broader, more systemic understandings of creativity beyond industrial models. These frameworks emphasise networks, collaboration, sustainability, and cultural rights, often in response to critiques of the instrumentalisation of culture and the exclusion of non-commercial practices. However, their practical implementation in cultural policymaking, particularly in contexts such as the Western Balkans, remains fragmented. As Dragicevic Sesic (n.d.) warns, such frameworks often overlook structural inequalities in global cultural trade and fail to address the asymmetries faced by culturally and economically marginalised regions.

In sum, while the CCI concept has enabled greater integration of culture within economic policy, its application needs to remain sensitive to contextual differences. Particularly in regions like the Western Balkans, inclusive and locally grounded cultural policies are essential to ensure that creativity serves not only markets but also democratic, social, and cultural development.

Models of CCI

Classification frameworks of the CCI have been continuously developing since the initial model in the UK, which was a subject to number of critiques. These frameworks now include criteria related to aesthetics, industrialisation, technical advancement, engagement of the creative labour, etc. (Throsby, 2008; Hesmondhalgh, 2002). In response to criticisms, the National Endowment for Science, Technology, and the Arts (NESTA) in 2006 and the Work

Foundation in 2007 developed two similar models that offer a more coherent and comprehensive understanding of creative industries, emphasising their complexity (National Endowment for Science, Technology and the Arts, 2006; Work Foundation, 2007). Both are based on concentric circles model of the creative industries, further elaborated by Throsby, (See Figure 2.1). It demonstrates different levels of cultural content in relation to economic value. In contrast, other circles emphasise the differentiation between core and periphery industries (Throsby, 2008).

According to this concept, the core circle consists of creative arts representing the highest cultural content. Nearby to this central focus are additional fundamental cultural sectors, which actively participate in commercial actions. Beyond that, there are the broader cultural industries where the financial value becomes more important than the cultural content. The furthest circle is mostly focused on commercial activities and has limited cultural content. This model aims to emphasise the diverse levels of cultural and economic importance in various sectors, therefore helping the creation and execution of detailed cultural strategies. This model shows that as one moves

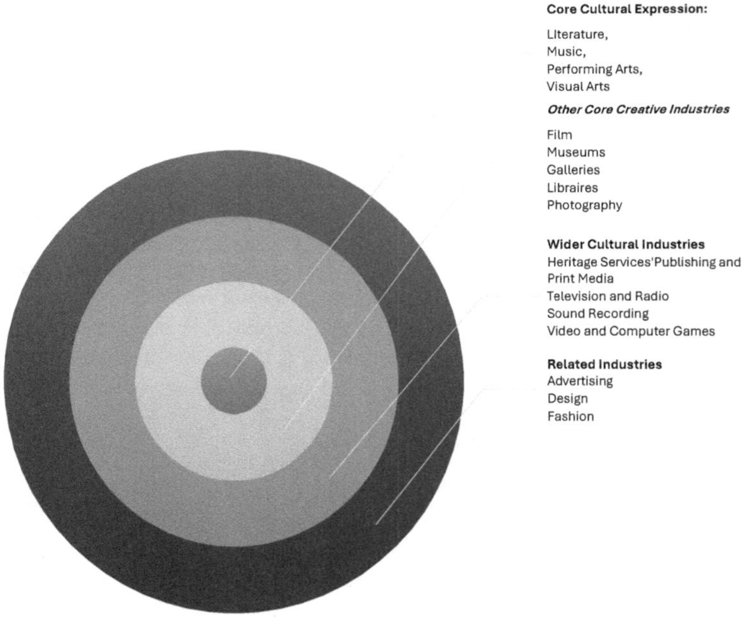

Figure 2.1 David Trosby concentric circles model

(*Source*: David Trosby 2008)

away from the fundamental creative fields of arts into allied industries, the share of creative labour and cultural content decreases (Throsby, 2008).

This model was later adopted and contextualised in many countries, including EU member-states, Asia, China, and the USA.

UNESCO and UNCTAD Perspectives

Over the past few decades, global organisations like the UNESCO and the UNCTAD have adopted the concept of CCIs. These institutions recognise creativity as a critical resource for fostering sustainable, human-centred development. UNESCO, in particular, has been instrumental in promoting policies that link culture with development, especially in underdeveloped regions such as the Western Balkans. Since the 1970s, UNESCO has advocated the idea that culture can be instrumental achieving political autonomy and economic empowerment in these regions (UNESCO, 2006).

One of the key actions and initiatives introduced by UNESCO is 2005 Convention on the Protection and Promotion of the Diversity of Cultural Expressions. The idea of this framework encourages policies that support CCIs at national and local levels while advocating for a fairer global distribution of cultural content, goods, and services. Another initiative introduced in 2009 was Cultural Statistics Framework which provides more accurate data on CCI in a globalised and technologically advanced world (UNESCO Institute for Statistics, 2009). However, despite this effort, challenges in gathering comparable, relevant data across different countries persist.

While UNESCO prioritises the social elements of culture, such as promoting diversity and equality, UNCTAD has focused more on the economic impact of CCIs (Flew, 2012). UNESCO's definition of cultural industries typically includes sectors like publishing, audio-visual production, crafts, and design, which are centred on the production of intangible cultural content. From the other side, UNCTAD's broader definition of creative industries includes both artistic sectors and those where creativity plays a key role in generating economic value, such as architecture and advertising (UNESCO, 2006; UNESCO Institute for Statistics, 2009).

UNCTAD has developed a model for the creative industries that includes broad spectrum of activities, from traditional arts to digital content creation, such as gaming (See Figure 2.2). This model highlights the economic potential of these industries to generate revenue through intellectual property and trade, thus positioning them as key drivers of development (United Nations Conference on Trade and Development, 2010).

These industries, built on innovation and creativity, are seen by UNCTAD as crucial in achieving the 2030 Agenda for Sustainable Development, proposed by the United Nations. However, developing countries, particularly those in regions like the Western Balkans, face significant challenges in fully integrating these models into their economies.

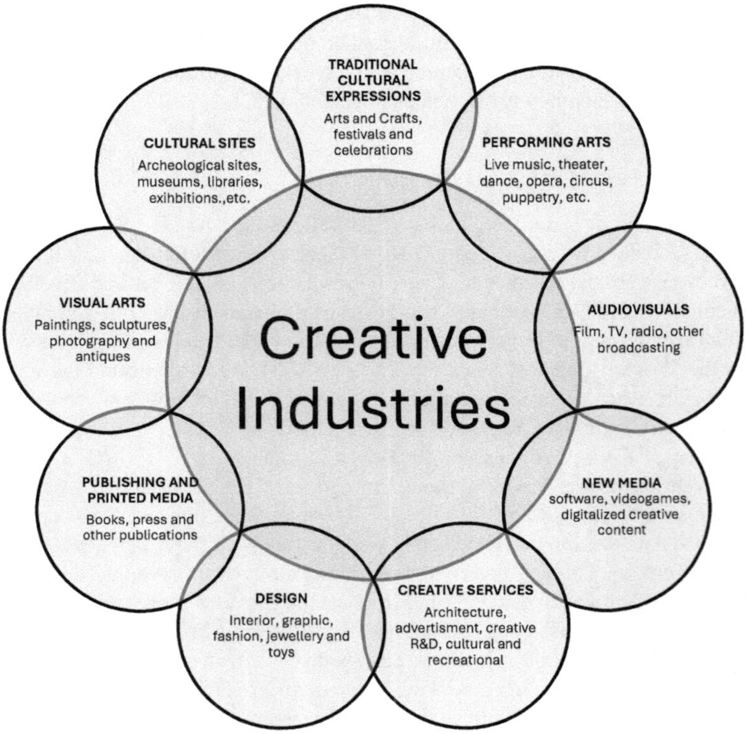

Figure 2.2 UNCTAD model of Creative Industries

Source: UNCTAD, Creative economy report 2010, p. 10, retreived August 12 2024

Development of Cultural and Creative Industries in the Western Balkans

The contemporary understanding of the CCI in the Western Balkans is deeply influenced by the socialist (communist) heritage from former Yugoslavia and Albania, where culture and creativity were viewed as non-profit sectors heavily subsidised and instrumentalised by the public authorities with very few opportunities for independent or private cultural and creative initiatives. After the conflict in former Yugoslavia and the dethrone of Enver Hoxha in Albania during the 1990s, when the old political, social, economic, and cultural systems started to be reconstructed into a new neoliberal and democratic one, based on western principles, there was a reinforcement of cultural activities and the establishment of new creative private companies, non-governmental, and not-for-profit organisations.

Throughout the transition from a socialist framework to a neoliberal, market-oriented democracy, CCI in the Western Balkans have assumed a distinctive role compared to their Western counterparts. It would be reductive to consider the development of CCI in the region without acknowledging their complex entanglement with the conflicts of the 1990s. On one hand, certain segments of the cultural sector, particularly popular media, literature, and music genres such as turbo folk, were actively instrumentalised by political regimes. These forms not only perpetuated nationalist narratives but also reinforced stereotypes, legitimised violence, and served as ideological tools that fuelled interethnic divisions. As Baker (2007) points out, turbo folk operated as a cultural category loaded with associations of violence, banality, and otherness, facilitating a framework through which the "other" was distanced and vilified. This culture industry was not only state-supported but also highly commercialised, allowing certain artists to thrive under the protection and patronage of political elites.

However, it is of great importance to recognise that even at the height of conflict, independent culture and arts, civil society sector, served as one of the few remaining forms of communication and connection between divided communities. Despite deep political ruptures, artistic and creative exchanges continued to exist across borders, often informally and outside official institutional channels. Independent theatre groups, visual artists, underground musicians, and film-makers engaged in efforts that defied nationalistic boundaries and fostered dialogue when political discourse had collapsed (Petrović, 2014). These counter-cultural movements functioned as spaces of resistance, preserving alternative narratives and upholding humanist values in times of violence and propaganda.

This duality reveals a defining characteristic of CCI in transitional contexts like the Western Balkans: the sector's importance has been more deeply rooted in its social and political role than its economic value (Dragićević Šešić, 2011a; Tomka, 2016). Artists outside the dominant, politically supported cultural discourse struggled to survive in conditions of international isolation, shrinking public funding, and institutional neglect (Lukić & Živković, 2017; Sretenović, 2013). Their perseverance underscores the resilience of creative communities and highlights the capacity of culture not only to divide, but also to connect and heal fractured societies (Luthar & Pušnik, 2010; Jović, 2009).

Recognising this complexity is essential for a balanced understanding of CCI in the Western Balkans. Acknowledging both their misuses and their role in maintaining communication during periods of fragmentation challenges simplified narratives of culture as either inherently progressive or regressive. It also offers a more nuanced foundation for contemporary policy development that honours the sector's layered history and its enduring relevance in promoting dialogue, solidarity, and inclusive democratic futures.

All Western Balkans countries, with great support from the international bodies, such as the British Council, UNESCO, European Commission, foreign embassies in the countries, etc., have recognised the importance of the CCI in their potential for creation of jobs and, in general, for its positive social and economic impact. Festivals, art biennales, preforming arts events, crafts, design, architecture, and publishing became important places where local talents were shown and where international audiences and attention were attracted. The creative community in the Western Balkans has also been influenced by digitalisation and technological breakthroughs, which have enabled some artists and creative people to have enhanced access to the global market and to explore another form of self-expression. The rise of film production, gaming, and digital media emphasised the possibility of the Western Balkans region for further development. However, despite these positive shifts and trends, many challenges related to CCI in the Western Balkans persist.

The field of CCI in the Western Balkans is exceptionally diverse but remains largely under-defined, with fragmented and often inconsistent approaches to its mapping and analysis. Although some attempts have been made to understand the scope and dynamics of the sector, the current body of knowledge is still limited and underdeveloped. As Cuff and Zečević (2022) note, data collection across the region lacks uniformity, with outdated or inconsistent methodologies and indicators used to measure sector performance. This deficiency in coherent research frameworks has contributed to a serious gap in knowledge production, making it difficult to understand the full economic, social, and cultural potential of the CCI sector. Much of the existing scholarship stems from economic, management, and business perspectives, often neglecting deeper cultural, sociological, and political dimensions (Cvetičanin, 2023; Judah & Vračić, 2019). This imbalance limits the potential to interpret CCIs as complex social ecosystems embedded in specific post-socialist, post-conflict, and transitional contexts (Grodach et al., 2023). Despite the evident lack of relevant and systematic research in the CCI sector, there are nevertheless some positive examples that suggest progress and could serve as a generator for strengthening the research field. The study by Cvetičanin et al. (2024), on unified research framework in cultural participation studies, offers a rare example of how cross-national research can be translated into regionally applicable insights and methodologies. Similarly, Grodach et al. (2023) stress the importance of local contexts in shaping creative economies and advocate for more inclusive, territorially grounded research approaches.

A further limitation lies in the absence of reliable, integrated statistical systems that could support policy interventions with evidence-based analysis. Research by the OECD (2024) highlights that while some countries in the region, such as Serbia, Albania, and North Macedonia, have initiated partial mapping or statistical exercises, these efforts remain fragmented and unaligned with international frameworks such as UNESCO's 2009 cultural statistics or Eurostat methodologies (Simjanovska, 2022). The disconnect between institutions, cultural practitioners, and statisticians, as described by Cvetičanin in interviews and analyses (Cvetičanin, 2023), further reinforces the need for frameworks that are not only methodologically rigorous but also contextually informed.

The creation of money and the creation of jobs are examples of economic benefits that are essential and serve as a motivation for the development of CCI. However, these benefits do not constitute the primary aim of the same industries in most of the countries in the Western Balkans region. The CCI in the Western Balkans are still mainly focused on shaping social dynamics and place a strong emphasis on social responsibility, more regularly prioritising it over economic benefit. According to Švob-Đokić (2005), the idea of CCI in the Western Balkans, particularly during the time of transition (1990s–2000s), is associated with the cultural creations that are associated with growing methods that revolve around free markets. Švob-Đokić argues that the process of turning the cultural creation towards market orientation entails a substantial change in the social status of cultural creation as well as redefining of the wider cultural system and values. At this point in time, the shifting viewpoints on the perception, understanding of the production, distribution, and consumption of cultural contents and services are still in the process of transitioning in the Western Balkans. A considerable number of artists and creative professionals, as well as decision-makers, still maintain traditional perspectives on culture and arts. The capacity of artists to interpret diverse ideas and traditions remains crucial, as demonstrated by their historical contributions to perception and innovation. There is a tendency for them to neglect the economic issues while putting an emphasis on the intrinsic and social qualities. Further, Primorac (2006, 2014) highlights that creative industries are inherently tied to profit-making through the creation and dissemination of symbolic goods. This provides a deeper understanding of the status of CCI in Southeast Europe, particularly in the Western Balkans. Primorac emphasises that, despite efforts to stimulate this sector with independent resources, the state remains a critical player in supporting this fragile industry (Primorac, 2014). The state is not only the major player in the creative industries sector, but it also effectively distances the concept itself from the original notions of independence, sustainability, and market orientation by articulating it specifically in state policies.

An additional set of important issues linked to the CCI in this region includes the cultural identity of the region and the impact of globalisation. Barnett and Lee (2002) describe globalisation as this intricate circulation of people, goods, profits, and symbols, which not only impacts economies but also reshapes cultures, societies, and the way symbolic meanings are communicated globally. Jovičić and Mikić (2006) point out the danger faced by small countries in this globalised world, such as those in the Western Balkans, which risk being dominated by imported cultural representations and meanings from other societies if they do not develop their own CCI. Both authors argue that long-term presence of such content can lead to an identity problem and problems with people's functioning in the immediate and wider environment (e.g., migration). The identity of the local population in this region is evidently affected by the soap operas broadcasted on public national and local TV services, predominantly originating from the Turkish-speaking region and featuring languages such as Spanish and English. In the absence of TV productions in local languages, Turkish series, Spanish, English and, in some countries, Russian, dominate the Balkan discourse. Given that television continues to have a significant role in the consumption of visual artistic expressions in the Balkans, TV series, entertainment programmes, and advertisements continue to hold an influential place in the everyday lives of viewers. Hancıgàz and Hülür (2024) found in their research, relevant to the Western Balkans region, that perception and attitude change among viewers because of television series. They discovered that media, particularly television series, significantly contribute to the creation or reshaping of identity. Therefore, in the Balkans, the frequent consumption of these soap series influences the usage of Turkish, Spanish, or Russian languages, in addition to English, in the everyday lives of individuals and contributes to the formation of discourse based on the principles and values coming from these productions.

The other important aspect of the overall situation with the CCI is the economic and political situation of the Western Balkans countries. Even though there was optimism for joining EU and adopting and harmonising with its legislation, there are still some challenges relating to adopting the democratic values and principles. In addition, the Western Balkans continue to face considerable challenges in the implementation of their development plans and strategies, including reforms in many fields, such as culture, education, health, social affairs, etc. In addition to this, the region is witnessing a rise in authoritarian leadership and stricter control, directly impacting the strategic direction of its countries. The reforms in the economic field have long been postponed, as Western Balkans economies face challenges in competing within the EU's common market. In accordance with the findings of Marku and Teqja (2024), a significant portion of the economies in the Western Balkans continue to be underdeveloped and are reliant on external financial support, loans, and help from the diaspora.

The current economic situation, the gross domestic product per capita in the six states that make up the Western Balkans is still only less than half of what it is in the European Union states (See Figure 2.3).

According to available data from Eurostat (2024), the projected GDP per capita for 2023 in Albania is 5.390 €, in Bosnia and Herzegovina it is 7.856 €, in Kosovo it is 5.920 €, in Montenegro it is 9.600 €, in North Macedonia it is 6.440 €, and in Serbia it is the highest at 10.500 € per capita. However, after decades of decline or stagnation, the Western Balkan countries saw economic growth, which was rebounded strongly in 2021 (World Bank Group, 2024a, 2024b). Montenegro (13%) and Kosovo (10,7%) experienced double-digit growth rates, while North Macedonia (4,5%) made more modest progress. The economic recovery was influenced by factors

Figure 2.3 Gross domestic products per capita at current market prices in the Western Balkan Countries, 2023

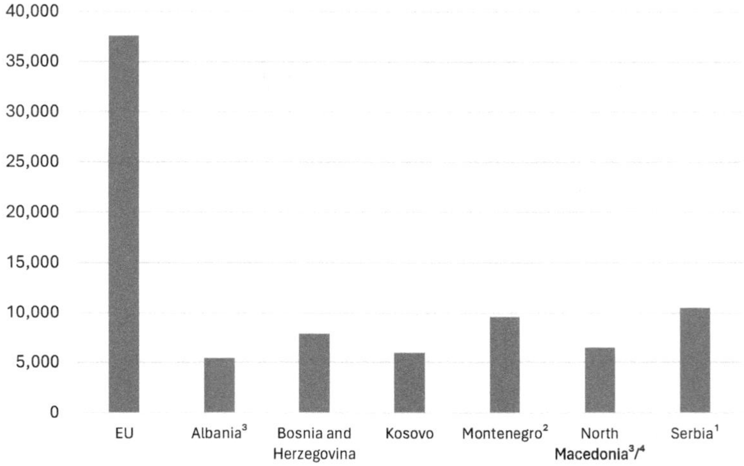

such as rise of exports, increased foreign investments, and increased private spending. By the end of 2023, the real GDP levels in all Western Balkan countries had significantly exceeded the levels before the pandemic (World Bank Group, 2024a, 2024b).

The labour market in the Western Balkans countries improved since 2016; however, 2024 shows early signs of stagnation. Unemployment rates have declined similarly across all countries, reducing the overall figure to 10.9%. Although the statistics indicate progress in this field, the reality is that there is a pressing need for skilled workers to sustain the economy, as a significant number of individuals are migrating to EU nations in search of better opportunities.

The poverty in this region declined in the past decade from nearly 30% to 15% in 2024. Between 2023 and 2025, poverty reduction is expected to drop from about 3% per year (World Bank Group, 2024a, 2024b).

These figures indicate that the overall political, social, and economic situation in the Western Balkans is still evolving and remains incomparable to that of other EU countries. This disparity directly affects the region's competitiveness and readiness for integration into EU markets, a reality that also extends to the CCI sector.

The cultural market is becoming another increasingly important issue, when taking into consideration CCI in the Western Balkans from the economic perspective. The concentration of markets on global level threatened the creative economy in the Western Balkans countries. According to the data from the United Nations Conference on Trade and Development (2024), four nations, namely the USA, China, the United Kingdom, and France, dominate

Figure 2.4 Global share of art market sales by value for 2023

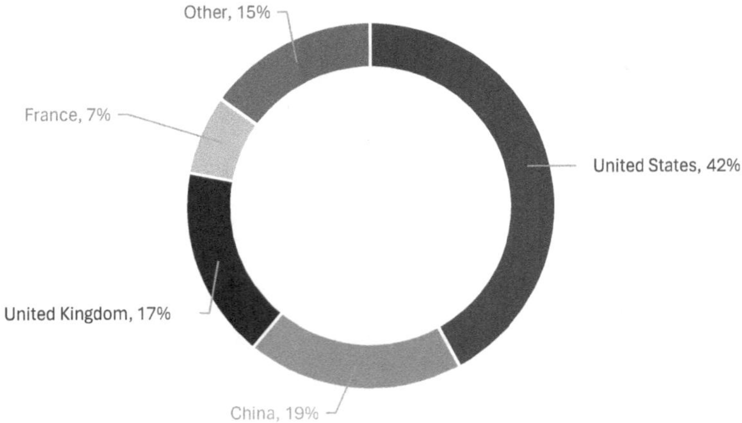

the worldwide arts market in regard to sales value, together accounting for 85% of the market (See Figure 2.4). The USA holds the largest share at 42%, followed by China at 19%, the United Kingdom at 17%, and France at 7%. The remaining 15% of the global art market was distributed to all other nations worldwide, including those in the Western Balkans group.

Dominant stakeholders on global level, in each sub sector of the CCI, negatively influence the smaller industries and the economies in their respective countries. The national markets in the Western Balkans countries are heavily influenced by global cultural industries, which weaken the competitiveness of domestic producers. These countries find themselves in an inferior position as importers and consumers due to their small cultural markets. The CCI industries in this region often operate in unregulated and unstable markets, leading to a focus on low-quality and low-volume cultural production to survive. In addition, the limited size and development of the domestic market in countries similar to those in the Western Balkans make it challenging for cultural products in the local language to be profitable. The technology is mostly outdated, and the products are not sufficiently competitive outside the region. As a result, domestic producers often become technical partners in international co-productions or create content for foreign markets in other languages. An exception to the generalisation about the CCI in the Western Balkans is the gaming industry, which demonstrates positive trends, along with a few isolated successes in other subsectors (Simjanovska, 2022).

The copyright issue and the legislative frameworks that are currently in place are another challenging matter. A small number of well-known artists and corporations receive a disproportionate number of profits from the existing copyright systems in the Western Balkans, which does not appropriately assist all artists. Having such a dominant position in the public realm suppresses diversity and is disadvantageous to the interests of most producers.

Despite the persistent political, economic, and cultural challenges in the Western Balkans, the CCI present potential for regional development. However, most of the governments in the Western Balkans still play a passive role towards the CCI, emphasising the market-oriented approach, without any serious analyses, plans, investments, or even understanding of the nature and needs of the CCI. The main governmental body responsible for the cultural and creative sectors in the Western Balkans is usually the Ministry of Culture, which usually includes public institutions, such as Film Agencies, National Libraries, Archives, National Theatres, and Art Galleries, that manages different subsectors. All these responsible public bodies have different understanding, approach and actions, mainly leaving the sector without explicit policy or clear priority in their agendas (Cuff & Zečević, 2022).

Even with all these challenges and weaknesses in the CCI, this region offers good examples and practices, achieving great visibility and success locally and internationally, socially, and economically. Several good examples are provided in Chapter 4, and one of them is the gaming industry. Traditionally dominated by North America, Japan, and the countries of the EU, this industry has experienced significant shifts in recent years. Specifically, the Western Balkans has appeared as a significant player in the industry. The region is not only contributing to the creation of best-selling games but also stimulating its cultural recognition and economic influence globally. Gaming, with all its subsectors, has evolved into a feasible career path for young people, offering opportunities that did not exist just a decade ago.

One of the most prominent examples is Nordeus, a Belgrade-based gaming company best known for developing *Top Eleven*, one of the world's most successful football management games with millions of users worldwide. Founded in 2010 by former Microsoft employees, Nordeus quickly rose to prominence in the mobile gaming industry. In 2021, the company was acquired by Take-Two Interactive for up to $378 million, marking one of the largest deals in Serbia's digital economy (Kuzmanova, 2021). Beyond its commercial success, Nordeus has actively invested in developing the local gaming ecosystem, co-founding the Serbian Games Association and launching the Nordeus Foundation to support education and digital empowerment in Serbia (Sabo, 2022). These initiatives demonstrate how the gaming industry in the Western Balkans is not only generating economic value but also contributing to social development and youth empowerment.

To summarise, great potential exists within the CCI sector in the Western Balkans; however, it is not yet developed properly. All the players in the CCI eco-system, including policymakers, lack clear efforts in making investments in areas such as research, capacity building, innovation, infrastructure, digitalisation, sustainability, and international and cross-border cooperation.

Although there are similarities in the understanding of the CCI in the Western Balkans, all countries in this region have individual approach to the CCI, therefore, this section is followed by an analysis of the CCI environment in each of the Western Balkans's countries, focusing on their distinct context.

A Country-by-Country Analysis of Cultural and Creative Growth in the Western Balkans

Analysing the CCI sector in the Western Balkans, including its respective subsectors, presents significant challenges. The key factors contributing for these challenges are the lack of a common understanding and definition of the CCI sector within the Western Balkans, insufficient and inadequate data collection and practices, and outdated statistical classification within the respective countries. Consequently, this chapter conducts analyses and presents the CCI status on a country-by-country basis, utilising the available data. From a methodological perspective, there are also significant challenges, including data insufficiency and the impracticality of applying a single methodology uniformly across all countries. The structural framework remains consistent across countries in this section; however, there is a notable inconsistency in the data availability, particularly with respect to the specific area, country, and dates of the available data.

Albania

The Demographic and Socio-Political Context of Albania

According to the 2023 Population and Housing Census conducted by the Institute of Statistics of Albania (INSTAT), the resident population of Albania is 2,402,113, marking a significant decrease from the 2011 census figure of 2,831,741 (Institute of Statistics of Albania, 2024b). (See Figure 2.5). Albania is a multicultural and multi-confessional country, with a religious composition comprising 45.86% Sunni Muslims, 4.81% Bektashi Muslims, 8.38% Catholics, 7.22% Eastern Orthodox, 0.4% Evangelicals, 0.15% adherents of other religions, 13.82% believers without denomination, 3.55% atheists, and 15.76% of the population not providing an answer (INSTAT, 2024).

Before 1991, Albania's communist regime controlled the entire political, social, and economical situation through centrally planned five-year strategies. The state owned all production assets, with fully collectivised agricultural and nationalised industries and complete instrumentalisation of the cultural field. Private business activities were prohibited, and a constitutional clause barred the government from seeking foreign aid, loans, or investment, contributing to the country's isolationist image. After the fall of Enver Hoxha, Albania dramatically shifted its strategic orientation towards the neoliberal concept of democratic societies. This fundamental political, social, and economic transformation of Albania was strongly supported by

Figure 2.5 Map of Albania

Source: Google Maps. Screenshot was taken from Google map from [https://www.google.com/search?q=google+map+for+Albania&oq=google+map+for+Albania&gs_lcrp=EgZjaHJvbWUyBggAEEUYOTIICAEQABgWGB4yCAgCEAAYFhgeMggIAxAAGBYYHjIICAQQABgWGB4yCggFEAAYDxgWGB4yCAgGEAAYFhgeMggIBxAAGBYYHjIICAgQABgWGB4yCAgJEAAYFhge0gEJNjcwMmowajE1qAIIsAIB&sourceid=chrome&ie=UTF-8]

the international community, primarily the USA, the EU, and the International Monetary Fund (IMF).

During this period of transition, Albania has made significant progress. From being the poorest country in the region, it has become an advanced middle-income economy.

With the opening up from the previously very rigid regime, and with interventions in the infrastructure, which was previously in a desperate state, it has become a very important tourist destination, especially in the last few years, attracting 6.8 million visitors in 2022 with projected revenues exceeding €3.04 billion (Shahidsaless et al., 2023).

A key process in this rapid transition of Albania is the EU integration, which formally became a candidate country for the EU in 2014. A significant year in this integration process for Albania is 2024, when the European Council adopted a European Partnership with Albania (European Commission, n.d.-a, n.d.-b).

Overview of the Cultural and Creative Sector in Albania

Since the establishment of the first Ministry of Culture in 2013, sincere efforts have been made in Albania to draft, refine, and implement progressive cultural policies. The current framework in relation to CCIs is in the National Strategy for Culture 2019–2025 (Ministry of Economy, Culture, and Innovation, 2019). According to this document, the main focus is oriented towards cultural heritage and its impact in driving sustainable development, followed by enhancing cultural infrastructure, positioning culture as a leading contributor to sustainable development. There is also a section of this strategy dedicated to CCI, in which there is a general commitment to developing these industries, without a clear action plan. The strategy also underscores the importance of developing entrepreneurial skills among artists and diversifying funding sources.

The key initiatives and projects, outlined in the strategy (2019–2025), aim to foster the growth of CCI, which also includes legislative reforms such as redefining the laws on art, culture, cinematography, and copyright. Key actions in this strategy include the rehabilitation of architectural heritage through programmes like "Heritage – Development Engine," establishment of new museums, and digitisation of cultural assets. The strategy also emphasises international promotion of Albanian, infrastructure improvements, such as constructing new cultural buildings and implementing e-ticketing systems for cultural sites (Ministry of Economy, Culture, and Innovation, 2019).

Despite these advancements, challenges persist when it comes to planning a new strategy, and even more so when implementation of these strategies or policy papers is underway. Some of these challenges include the lack of relevant research and data (classification, statistics) about the CCI, the need for improved intersectoral coordination, stronger support of independent artists and organisations, a clearer legislative framework, and greater integration of technology in cultural products.

Economic Contribution of the CCI

According to UNESCO (2020), in Albania, the CCI's contribution to the country's Gross Domestic Product (GDP) accounts for 2.95% of the overall GDP. This indicates that cultural activities and industries serve as an important economic driver.

In 2021, cultural employment in Albania accounts 21,078 individuals, which represents 1.7% of the country's total workforce. The data also reveals a gender disparity within the cultural workforce, with men comprising the majority at 58.3% (Institute of Statistics of Albania, 2021).

According to the Albanian Institute for Statistics, in 2023, public expenditures on Entertainment, Culture, and Religious Affairs constituted 1.75% of the total public expenditures and represented 0.51% of the total GDP. This indicates that less priority is being given to these sectors, relative to the overall economy and total public budget (Institute of Statistics of Albania 2021).

Exports and International Presence

Based on the available data, Albania's world trade in 2023 included €8.3 billion worth of imports and €4.1 billion exports valued. In relation to the European

Union (EU27), Albania exported €4.2 billion worth of goods, while imports from the EU amounted to €2.8 billion. This indicates a strong export capacity and reliance on the European market. It is important to note that these figures include all industries, while data on cultural goods is limited (European Commission, n.d.-a, n.d.-b).

Moreover, the domestic consumption of cultural goods and services constitutes 3.1% of Albanian overall household consumption expenditure (UNESCO, 2020). This figure emphasises the value of cultural products in the everyday lives of Albanian citizens, reflecting households' notable investment in cultural activities and services (UNESCO, 2020).

Spotlight on Albania's Leading Creative Industries

Film and Cinema

Despite Albania's isolationist policies, the country generated and produced in average 13 film annually from 1975–1990. Following the dissolution of Communism in 1991, the film industry faced significant challenges, resulting in a dramatic decrease in productivity with hardly one or two films made each year. The Albanian National Centre of Cinematography was established in 1997 to revitalise the industry by facilitating funding schemes for films as well as stimulating international collaboration. Events such as the Tirana International Festival and Dea Film Festival have significantly contributed to the promotion of the Albanian cinema (Albanian National Center of Cinematography, n.d.).

Art and Design

The National Gallery of Arts in Albania is one of the most important cultural points, housing over 5,000 artworks and maintaining records of 600 registered artists in its archives (Visit Tirana, n.d.). While its permanent collection predominantly features Socialist Realism, the gallery has also showcased works by renowned Albanian and international artists through various exhibitions. Core elements of the gallery's mission are its educational programmes, which engage numerous children and students, fostering an appreciation for the arts.

Albania's cultural art and heritage is further represented by its 12 museums, castles, and monuments, alongside seven archaeological parks, which collectively attracted 1,005,815 visitors in 2023 (Institute of Statistics of Albania, 2023). In terms of creative industries, the first graphic design studios emerged post-1990s in response to the business demand for advertising and promotional materials, though the market remains relatively small. Nonetheless, the sector has seen the rise of several dynamic agencies specialising in graphic design, advertising, branding, and digital media, including Kilica Studio (Studio Kilica, n.d.), Delta Print Studio (n.d.), and Albdesign (n.d.).

Fashion

The fashion industry in Albania has a relatively small market. However, this industry garnered attention, leading to the opening of numerous training programmes for young individuals to acquire skills and pursue careers in this field. In 2017, Art Kontakt, an Albanian cultural organisation that deals with contemporary arts, organised several training programmes for young fashion designers, bringing together students, curators, and design specialists for discussions at Art Kontakt (n.d.). Many Albanian designers have pursued independent careers, showcasing their collections and participating in events such as Albania Fashion Week (AFW), which plays an important role. The event annually brings together designers, stylists, textile manufacturers, models, and makeup artists to showcase ready-to-wear collections to the Albanian public. Despite the limited market size, the number of designers is relatively high, including notable figures such as Joni Peci, Enada At Nikolla, Stela Sallaku, Mirela Nurce, Rezarta Skifteri, Bukuroshe Sinanaj, etc.

Music and Performing Arts

The Albanian music business is marked by a dynamic and diverse music landscape, firmly linked to traditional folk music, and yet progressively shaped by modern global influences. UNESCO has recognised traditional Albanian music, particularly iso-polyphony, as an intangible cultural heritage, highlighting its importance as local cultural expression.

This rich heritage coexists with modern genres such as pop, hip-hop, rock, and electronic music, which have gained popularity, especially among younger audiences.

The industry has seen substantial growth since the 1990s, with the emergence of music festivals such as Festivali i Këngës, Kënga Magjike, Jazz and Wine, Tirana Jazz Shkodra, Festival RockStock, the Festival "Maratona e Kenges Popullore", Top Fest, Paragliding Open Air Festival, Jog Festival, and the Festival of Classical Music "Maria Kraja." All of these music events provide platforms for artists to showcase their work and gain national and international recognition. Albania is not an isolated island in terms of digital transformation. Digital technologies and social media have transformed the Albania's music industry helping musicians and music professionals to expand their audience and promote independent music. Numerous musicians and professionals in the field struggle in accessing the worldwide music industry due to insufficient skills, especially in digital literacy, limited market size which is affected by the language barriers, inadequate infrastructure, and copyright and intellectual property issues. Another issue is the lack of adequate governmental support.

Dedicated to producing high-quality artistic theatre and promoting Albanian dramaturgy, the National Theatre of Albania is the foremost theatre institution in the country. Currently, the National Theatre operates from the "New Stage arTurbina" building, which houses two stages with capacities of 150 and 400 seats (European Theatre Convention, n.d.). In addition to the National Theatre, "Teatri Migjeni" (Teatri Migjeni, n.d.), there is another prominent Albanian theatre in Shkodra. The country also hosts significant theatre festivals, such as the Butrint International Theatre Festival which returns to the UNESCO World Heritage site Tirana Times (n.d.), and the Skampa Festival in Elbasan (Skampa International Theatre Festival, n.d.), which has recently expanded to Tirana, promoting contemporary theatrical trends and intercultural dialogue.

Digital and Gaming

The gaming industry in Albania is still in its nascent stages, characterised by a relatively small but growing community of developers, gamers, and enthusiasts. The country lacks a substantial infrastructure for large-scale game development, with most activity concentrated in small indie studios and freelance developers who often collaborate on international projects. Lack of legal framework and government as well as proper transcription programmes are the main obstacles in this industry (All Correct Games, n.d.).

Conclusion

Despite inadequate infrastructural and public support constrains, Albanian's CCI such as film, music, fashion, and gaming are gaining local and international attention, contributing at the same time to the development of the country. Initiatives coming from the public, private, and independent sector as well as the international collaboration and support play an extremely important role in developing this sector. With its extensive cultural legacy, vibrant young generation, and expending tourism sector, Albania is well located to emerge as a regional hub for CCI.

Bosnia and Herzegovina

The Demographic and Socio-Political Context of Bosnia and Herzegovina

The 2013 census in Bosnia and Herzegovina (See Figure 2.6) recorded a population of 3,531,159. The country is well known for its cultural, religious, and historical diversity, with official languages being Bosnian, Serbian, and Croatian.

As mentioned in the previous chapter, the governmental structure consists of Federation of Bosnia and Herzegovina, Republika Srpska, and autonomous Brčko District. Furthermore, the Federation comprises of 10 cantons and 79 municipalities, whereas Republika Srpska consists of 62 municipalities. The

Figure 2.6 Map of Bosnia and Herzegovina

Sources: Google Maps. Screenshot was taken from Google map from [https://maps.app.goo.gl/gpd5Da67DqE9yce49]

population distribution in these territories is as follows: the Federation has 2,219,220 residents (62.85%), Republika Srpska has 1,228,423 residents (34.79%), and Brčko District has 83,516 or (2.3%) of the total population.

Bosnia and Herzegovina was one of the most endangered countries during the conflict and war in the former Yugoslavia, suffering great losses, genocide, and traumas. All that chaos ended with the signing of the Dayton Peace Agreement (Organization for Security and Co-operation in Europe [OSCE], 2014). However, while this agreement established a framework for peace, it is still lacking functionality and presents significant challenges for the country's long-term development. The turning point for Bosnia and Herzegovina in this transition period is the EU integration process, which culminated with the obtaining of a candidate status in 2022 (European Commission, n.d.-c, n.d.-d).

The economy in this country, as in other Western Balkans countries, is classified as upper-middle-income, with a total GDP of €22.99 billion, with a GDP per capita of €7185.23 (World Bank, 2021). The most important sector in this economy is the service sector, which accounts for 55.7% of GDP and 50.3% of employment, followed by the industrial sector at 23.9% with 31.7% employment, and the agriculture sector, which accounts for 6.2% to GDP with 18% of the workforce (Organisation for Economic Co-operation and Development [OECD], 2022).

According to the data available, the major labour market indicators from 2021 show a 39.6% employment rate and 17.4% unemployment (United Nations Economic Commission for Europe, n.d.). For the same year, 16.9% of the population lives in relative poverty and 18.5% in absolute poverty (UNICEF, 2023).

Overview of the Cultural and Creative Sector in Bosnia and Herzegovina

Having in mind the complicated governmental structure for the cultural and creative sector in Bosnia and Herzegovina, as described in Chapter one, the CCI in this country faces significant challenges. Support structures remain fragmented, lacking cohesive coordination, which obstruct the development of a unified network for CCI within the country's complex state system (Kalender, 2014). Moreover, the protection of copyright, the limited internationalisation of the CCI, and the absence of sustainable and effective funding models for the sector represent significant challenges (Mikić, 2013). Furthermore, according to Havoli et al. (2023), the allocation for culture in the national budget, from 2010–2016, was restricted to approximately 1% of the total domestic expenditures, which indicated that this amount is inadequate for achieving all strategic objectives, especially those related to CCI.

Despite the challenges in the CCI in Bosnia and Herzegovina, numerous efforts by the public, private, and international organisations are actively advancing the development of CCI in the country. The country's major urban centre, Sarajevo, functions as a key hub for these industries. One notable initiative is the Sarajevo Film Fund, which provides support and resources for filmmakers in the region (Sarajevo City of Film, n.d.-a). Similarly, the Sarajevo UNESCO City of Film programme positively influences the cinematic development (Sarajevo City of Film, n.d.-b). In addition to these, BIT Alliance (n.d.-b), a prominent association supporting the IT industry, contributes significantly to the digital and technological advancements within the creative sector. Another interesting initiative is the AABAH creative hub, that provides physical space where young architects, designers, and other creative professionals collaborate together (Asocijacija arhitekata u Bosni i Hercegovini, n.d.). In addition, Banja Luka's Innovative Centre is another platform that supports and brings together young creative and innovative people (Innovation Centre Banja Luka, n.d.).

Economic Contribution of the CCI

Nurkovic (2015) conducted one of the few available studies on the development of the creative industries in Bosnia and Herzegovina, estimating that the sector's value added exceeds 10% of the national GDP. This aligns with findings presented by Mikić (2013), who reported that the value added by the CCI in Bosnia and Herzegovina is approximately 11.6%. These figures likely reflect a broader understanding of the CCI at that time.

The available data on cultural employment in Bosnia and Herzegovina is very limited. Although the existing data is outdated, it still offers a basic overview of the state of CCI in the country. According to Mikić (2013), 3,900 of entities in the CCI were registered, from which 24% publishing sector, 30% architecture and design, 15% marketing and advertising, and 7% Fashion design. More precise information is given in Nurkovic's (2015) research, where the number of entities is estimated to be 3,581 in 2011, with the architecture sector having the highest contribution in the share of the total number of creative industries, while video and multimedia have the lowest among the listed creative industries (See Figure 2.7).

The cultural employment accounts from 4.2% in 2003 to 6.44% in 2011, of the total workforce from which approximately 65% are engaged in core cultural activities and 35% in supporting roles Mikić (2013). While these figures highlight the significance of culture as an employment sector, they likely underestimate its overall contribution due to data limitations.

Figure 2.7 Number of entities in Creative Industries in Bosnia and Herzegovina (2011)

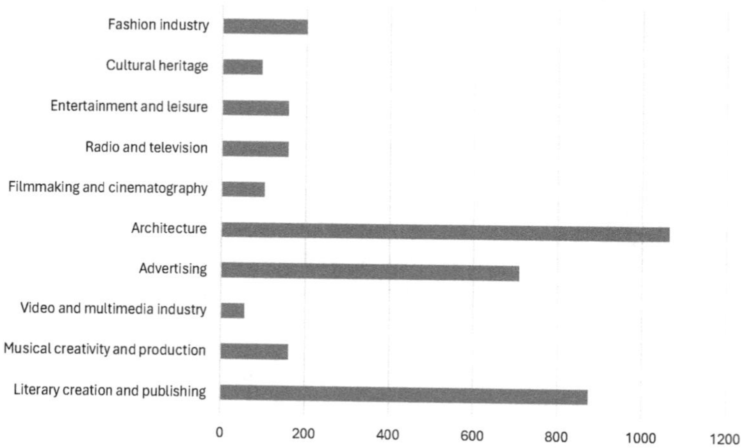

Exports and International Presence

According to Mikić (2013), the export value of the CCI in Bosnia and Herzegovina is estimated to be approximately 139,803,000 euros. In comparison, the import of cultural goods into the country stands at an estimated 117,179,000 euros. This data indicates a significant export gain in the cultural sector, suggesting that Bosnia and Herzegovina is actively engaging in the international cultural market, with its creative industries contributing significantly to the national economy. This export-import dynamic not only highlights the country's cultural assets but also underscores its potential to expand its influence in the global creative economy. These figures indicate that the CCI are the growing sector in the country with great potential.

Spotlight on Bosnia and Herzegovina's Leading Creative Industries

Film and Cinema

Sarajevo, the capital of Bosnia and Herzegovina, is one of the most important creative hubs in the country, with long history and success. The city has great legacy for film, as it has held a film school that, in 1970 and 1989, has shaped the Yugoslavian cinema. The Sarajevo film festival, outlined in Chapter 4, has become a global cultural event and helped build a vibrant cinema community in the country and in the region (Sarajevo Film Festival, n.d.). Bosnian filmmakers have achieved remarkable international success, earning prestigious awards such as the Academy Award and accolades from renowned film festivals including Cannes, Venice, and others. Danis Tanović's *No Man's Land* (2001) won the Academy Award for Best Foreign Language Film and also received the Best Screenplay Award at the Cannes Film Festival (Academy of Motion Picture Arts and Sciences, 2002; Festival de Cannes, n.d.-a). Jasmila Žbanić's *Quo Vadis, Aida?* (2020) premiered in competition at the Venice Film Festival and went on to be nominated for Best International Feature Film at the 93rd Academy Awards and Best Director at the BAFTA Awards (Academy of Motion Picture Arts and Sciences, 2021; La Biennale di Venezia, 2020). Aida Begić's debut feature *Snow* (2008) won the Grand Prix at Cannes' Critics' Week, while her later film *Children of Sarajevo* (2012) was awarded a Special Distinction in the Un Certain Regard section at Cannes (Semaine de la Critique, 2008; Festival de Cannes, n.d.-b). Additionally, the documentary *Miracle in Bosnia* (1995), directed by Dino Mustafić and Danis Tanović, received a Special Award at the Cannes Film Festival (Festival de Cannes, n.d.-c).

Another important initiative in this industry is the UNESCO Creative City of Film that helps the developing of local film infrastructure, which benefits both young and experienced filmmakers.

According to the Agency for Statistics of Bosnia and Herzegovina (2023), in 2022, the country had 37 cinemas, hosted 51,289 film screenings throughout the year, attracting a total of 437,653 visitors. These figures indicate a consistent involvement with cinematic culture, highlighting cinema's importance in the cultural and social life of Bosnia and Herzegovina.

Art and Design

An increase in the number of educational programmes in design and the expansion of this sector into publishing, production, classical, and new and digital media have all played a role in the emergence of a significant number of capable young designers. They mostly engage in freelance work, but there is also an emerging scene of small creative agencies and studios. A long tradition of the Graphic Design Department from the University has ensured a recognisable movement of Sarajevo design.

The Agency for Statistics of Bosnia and Herzegovina (2023) reported 18 museums and 19 galleries in 2022. Together, these institutions host 181 exhibitions. This indicates the active role of museums and galleries in the country's cultural life, hosting different kind of content, from historic to contemporary. In this subsector, the strong art education legacy facilitated the successful employment of a good number of formally trained artists in the creative sector.

Fashion

The fashion industry in Bosnia and Herzegovina is a relatively small, yet growing sector. It may not be as prominent as in other countries, but local designers and companies are gaining attention locally and internationally. Sarajevo and Mostar fashion weeks provide important platforms for designers.

Music and Performing Arts

Bosnia and Herzegovina's music scene is diverse, covering genres from traditional sevdalinka to pop, rock, jazz, and classical. Despite the strong musical education, there were only 14 professional orchestras and choirs in 2022, including two philharmonics in Sarajevo and Banja Luka, down from 30 ensembles in 2019 (Agency for Statistics of Bosnia and Herzegovina, 2023). In the same year, 696 concerts attracted 170,185 visitors (ibid).

The country has 29 theatres, 11 of which are professional, and an increasing number of independent theatre groups formed by young artists. As the only opera and ballet theatre in Sarajevo, the National Theatre is the most notable. However, while there aren't many independent or private theatres in Sarajevo, a growing number of young, educated performing artists are forming smaller, independent theatre ensembles and ad-hoc groups.

Among the several events that support the performing arts both locally and internationally are the Sarajevo Jazz Festival, International Theatre Festival Mess (MESS. n.d.), and Baščaršija Nights.

Digital and Gaming

An increasing number of tech start-ups and organisations focused on software development, digital design, and game development, together with the young and talented workforce, are the main characteristics of Bosnia and Herzegovina's digital and gaming industry.

Games made by local companies and independent developers are becoming famous all around the world. One of the most important organisations in this field is BITAlliance, founded in 2014 (Bit Alliance, n.d.-a). It is involved in education by helping, synchronising, and improving the current curriculum based on industry needs. In addition, this organisation is active in advocacy, improving the working conditions of this industry. It also hosts events, seminars, and training session, encouraging the expansion of the digital and game sector in the country. Another success story that came from Bosnia and Herzegovina is NSoft – A Mostar-based company that has developed a suite of virtual games and betting performs that are utilised in over 35 countries. Notably, NSoft was the only company from this country to be listed in Deloitte's Fast 50 competition, achieving a remarkable four-year growth rate of 1,760% and securing fifth position (NSoft, n.d.).

Conclusion

The CCI sector in Bosnia and Herzegovina is a dynamic and diverse field that plays an essential role in the country's identity and has some impact on the economy. Even though it is confronted with obstacles such as the complex and challenging governance structure, insufficient funding opportunities, old infrastructure, and small and fragmented market, the industry, such as the Film, has shown that it can be a generation for a serious social and economic development. For the CCI sector to fully realise its potential, there is a need for strategic investments, improved infrastructure, and stronger policy support.

Kosovo

The Demographic and Socio-Political Context of Kosovo

As of the year 2024, Kosovo, which is one of the smaller countries in the region, has a population of 1,586,695 (Kosovo Agency of Statistics, 2023).

Following the conflict in former Yugoslavia, Kosovo (See Figure 2.8) has faced serious challenges in terms of achieving and keeping political and economic stability. This is mainly due to the ongoing disagreement with Serbia, which still regards Kosovo as part of its territory. Despite all these challenges, Kosovo declared independence in 2008, and until this moment, 100 UN member countries have recognised its sovereignty (World Bank, 2024a).

Figure 2.8 Map of Kosovo

Source: Google Maps. Screenshot was taken from Google map from [https://maps.app.goo.gl/nU6Ykd4jWu2ZVpV16]

However, this issue remains unsolved, hindering diplomatic relations and limiting economic and cultural development. It complicates access to international markets and trade routes, as well as raises concerns about regional stability among potential investors. Negotiations to normalise this bilateral disagreement have been delayed, and the main reason for that is the lack of political will from both sides. An example of this complicated relationship is the wish and will coming from the prime minister of Kosovo, Albin Kurti, who is insisting on formal recognition of Kosovo from Serbia. On the other side, Serbia is opposing this requirement from Kosovo and is blocking its international participation in all major organisations and platforms. At the same time, EU has warned Serbia to stop impeding Kosovo's membership into key international bodies or risk jeopardising its EU aspirations (Turp-Balazs, 2024).

Resolving this issue and normalising the relations between Serbia and Kosovo will help Kosovo's international recognition and open new possibilities for trade, attract new investments, and influence positively the cultural regional and international cooperation. In addition, these tensions between these two countries will have positive impact on the entire region.

In the period after 2020, Kosovo is advancing its relations with the European Union, having the Stabilisation and Association Agreement, active since 2016, and in 2021 it has been part of the European Reform Agenda (Council of the European Union, 2015).

Kosovo's current economy is classified as middle-income with GDP of €9.98 billion and a GDP per capita of €5,630.37 (World Bank, 2024a). In 2023, the unemployment rate stood at 10.7%, while 23% of the population lived in poverty in 2021. Moreover, Kosovo's GDP per capita represents only one-quarter of the European Union average. These figures show that the country continues to face serious economic challenges.

Overview of the Cultural and Creative Sector in Kosovo

The darkest period of the cultural field in Kosovo was between 1989 and 1999 when complete shutdown of Kosovo's cultural institutions under the Serbian regime took place, also leading to the closure of educational facilities. In the same period, the president at that time, Ibrahim Rugova, initiated the establishment of new, parallel structures to preserve cultural and educational institutions, including the establishment of Kosovo Philharmonic Orchestra and restructuring of the educational system.

However, the real development of the cultural institutions in Kosovo began only after the parliamentary elections in 2001, with the establishment of provisional self-government institutions, including the Ministry of Culture, Youth, and Sports.

Despite the governmental efforts and in particular the related Ministry, culture remains marginalised in public discourse and policy. The lack of a coherent and explicit cultural policy or any strategy for cultural development, led to uncoordinated treatment of this field and an absence of strategic long-term planning. However, cultural organisations, such as Dokufest, A Film Festival in Prizren, have demonstrated resilience and have shown that even without a public support they can influence and inspire the community socially, culturally, and economically. One of the rare research projects on culture in Kosovo, the report by the GAP Institute (GAP Institute for Advanced Studies, 2012) has shown that Dokufest contributed €3.1 million to the local GDP in 2011, with projections of €21.9 million over the following four years. This festival has attracted approximately 10,000 visitors in 2013 and has influenced other festivals across Kosovo to strengthen their capacities and influence the cultural and economic landscape in the local communities.

Since 2021, the newly appointed Minister Hajrulla Çeku, with a background in the civil society sector and prior involvement in the cultural activism, has initiated numerous significant reform efforts to modernise the management of the culture system. Initially, he initiated a process for creating a preliminary version of the Strategy for Cultural Development of Kosovo. Additionally, he initiated the establishment of long-term financial grant schemes for independent art organisations, aimed at fostering their sustainable development.

Another important initiative that supports CCI in Kosovo is the Creative Industries project, initiated by the UNDP (United Nations Development Programme, n.d.), aiming at establishing a supporting environment for the creative economy. Another remarkable event, Manifesta 14 held in Prishtina 2022, significantly affected Kosovo's cultural, social, and urban and economic scene, thereby improving its worldwide profile by attracting 800,000 tourists (Manifesta 14, n.d.). Participation in this kind of initiatives mobilises all sectors, such as public, private, and independent, and creates an opportunity for further development of the entire CCI sector in Kosovo. This event drew the attention of both national and local decision-makers, as numerous infrastructure projects were involved in the preparation for this significant event. According to Swiss contact, "Manifesta 14 transforms Kosovo's capital into a 100-day exhibition venue." This project was also important for strengthening the regional cooperation, as many organisations from Serbia, North Macedonia, and Albania were involved (Swisscontact, 2022).

Despite the good practices and initiatives, there are some persisting challenges in the CCI sector. One of the key challenges in the CCI sector is the issue of statistics and data gathering in the cultural field. This poses a barrier for researchers to accurately assess the cultural, social, and economic impact (Breznica et al., 2024).

The other challenges that the CCI in Kosovo is facing are linked to limited funding and investments, lack of a clear policy framework, including the legislation, political and economic instability, limited access to international markets, educational and professional gaps, brain drain and limited opportunities for young people in the creative sector, a fragmented sector, and lack of regional and international collaboration.

Economic Contribution of the CCI

The absence of comprehensive data on the contribution of the CCI sector in Kosovo's economy highlights a critical gap in research. Although detailed statistics on the economic impact of CCI in Kosovo are scarce, studies from neighbouring countries in the Western Balkans suggest that the sector typically contributes between 2% and 5% to GDP. Given Kosovo's similar economic structure, it is plausible to assume that its CCI sector faces analogous growth constraints and opportunities.

From this general data available and the context in which CCI are operating in Kosovo, one can predict that the CCI contribution to the national GDP is relatively small compared to other sectors, reflecting the challenges of a transition economy and the situation with the cultural sector in the past transitional years. Legal and political uncertainties, a slow privatisation process, and limited investment incentives have contributed to this situation.

State-owned businesses and public services continue to have a big impact on Kosovo's economy, and they also have a big influence on the national budget. According to the International monetary fund (2023), the recent economic performance of Kosovo has been stable, with preliminary data indicating a real GDP growth rate of 3.5% for 2023. Key factors driving this growth include strong external demand, such as increased tourism from the diaspora and the emergence of IT and business service exports. This economic context reflects the broader challenges and opportunities for the CCI sector in Kosovo.

According to the Agency for Statistic in Kosovo, in 2022, 3,720 individuals were employed in cultural sectors or professions, constituting 0.9% of the total employment. The majority of those employed in cultural activities were men, accounting for 80.4% of the total, which represents a 0.4% decline from the previous year (Kosovo Agency of Statistics, 2023).

Exports and International Presence

Based on the limited data available about the contribution of CCI to exports and its international presence, some general comments on this aspect of Kosovo's economy are offered. The export sector is relatively small but expanding, predominantly comprising metals, minerals, and agricultural products, with the European Union – especially Germany and Italy – being the primary export markets. The country also engages in trade with regional partners such as Albania and North Macedonia. According to the International Trade Administration (2024), Kosovo faces a significant trade deficit, with exports accounting for only about 15.3% of total imports in 2022. The diaspora, whose financial contributions constitute nearly 15% of the GDP and significantly contribute to economic stability, heavily supports the country's economy, with increased diaspora tourism during the summer months (International Trade Administration, 2024).

Spotlight on Kosovo's Leading Creative Industries

Film and Cinema

Kosovo's film industry is a vibrant creative sector, with Kosovafilm being a key player, especially post-independence, producing short films, documentaries, cartoons, and features. Since 2008, the Kosova Cinematography Centre (KCC, n.d.) has been the central public film fund, supporting film production, distribution, and promoting Kosovo's cinema internationally. Investment in the industry has led to multiple international awards, including an Oscar nomination for the short film "Shok." DokuFest, Kosovo's premiere documentary and short film festival since 2002, has become a major cultural event, promoting creative exchange, boosting the local economy, and drawing thousands of visitors annually.

Art and Design

The major national institution in the visual art field is the Kosova National Art Gallery, established in 1979. It is named after Muslim Mulliqi, one of the most prominent Kosovar artists, with an aim to preserve and collect works of art. Since the independence, more than 300 individual and collective exhibitions of Kosovo and international artists have taken place (National Gallery of Kosovo, n.d.).

Kosovo's design industry is small, with new independent studios and start-ups specialising in graphic and digital design, web development, and branding. Events such as the REDO Prishtina, an annual international graphic design and visual arts event, provide platforms for designers to showcase their work and connect with both local and international audiences (ReDo Prishtina, 2024).

Fashion

The fashion industry is in the initial phase, gradually beginning to take shape and establish its presence. However, the availability of fashion design education in Kosovo is a positive development that can foster this industry and become a creative hub in the future (United Nations Development Programme, 2023).

Music and Performing Arts

The music industry in Kosovo is relatively well developed and its market is enlarged within the neighbouring countries Albania and North Macedonia because of the Albanian-speaking population. In addition to the international great success of Dua Lipa, a pop musician from Kosovo who is currently living in the UK, the domestic scene is vibrant, featuring numerous musicians and music professionals and diverse genres of music festivals and events. This music star has also been key factor in organising the Sunny Hill Festival (Sunny Hill Festival, n.d.), Kosovo's largest music event. This festival, which attracts some of the biggest names in the music world, has positioned Prishtina as one of the key destinations on the festival map in Southeast Europe.

The theatre field in Kosovo is vivid, internationally recognised, and internationally well linked. The leading institution in this field is The National Theatre in Prishtina that receives most of the national funding for the theatre sector in Kosovo. However, the theatre sector has emerging vibrant independent theatres that often outperform the National Theatre in terms of production volume and audience size. One of the most prominent independent theatres is ODA, which averages over 200 artistic events annually and welcomes approximately 50,000 visitors (ODA Theatre, n.d.). Unfortunately, the theatres located outside Prishtina, the capital of Kosovo, face challenges due to the unstable and limited public support, which downsizes their abilities to maintain a stable workforce and deliver high-quality production.

The National Ballet of Kosovo remains the primary institution for dance performances in the country.

Digital and Gaming

While the digital and gaming industry in Kosovo is still in the formation phase, it holds significant potential for economic development. The interest in the game design sector has witnessed a consistent upward trend in recent years. A growing number of individuals in Kosovo are increasingly viewing game design as a viable business opportunity. As reported by Kosovo 2.0, there was only one registered business involved in computer game publishing in 2012. However, by 2018, this figure had surged to 63 active businesses (Guri, 2019).

Conclusion

The CCI in Kosovo, while still in a developing phase, holds significant potential for economic and social impact. Despite challenges such as political instability due to the unsolved issue with Serbia, limited funding, insufficient infrastructure, and a lack of comprehensive policy support, sectors like music, film, design, visual art, and independent theatre are showing promising growth and increasing visibility both locally and internationally. Key cultural events, such as DokuFest, Manifesta 14, and the Sunny Hill Festival, along with emerging digital and gaming initiatives, highlight the dynamic creativity of Kosovo's youth and the sector's capacity to drive innovation and cultural diplomacy.

Montenegro

The Demographic and Socio-Political Context of Montenegro

Montenegro (See Figure 2.9) is the smallest Western Balkans country with 623,633 inhabitants (Statistical Office of Montenegro, 2024). It is a multi-ethnic country with an ethnic composition of 41.12% Montenegrins, 32.93% Serbs, 9.45% Bosniaks, 4.97% Albanians, 2.06% Russians, and 1.67% Muslims (Statistical Office of Montenegro, 2024). In the last several years, Montenegro's demographic map has undergone significant changes, particularly since the war in Ukraine started. Over 62,000 Ukrainians have arrived in Montenegro, while 24,958 remain in the country, with 6,118 of them having applied for temporary protection (as of 22 August 2022). In addition, over 14,000 Russians are residing in Montenegro, as of August 2022 (United Nations, 2022). These changes affect the everyday life of the citizens; however, no clear policy of how to tackle this issue is still visible.

Figure 2.9 Map of Montenegro

Source: Google Maps. Screenshot was taken from Google map from [https://maps.app.goo.gl/cdy7MHbX9xE6L3mw9]

Montenegro is a country with a complex history, gaining its independence in 2006, after splitting from the federation of Serbia & Montenegro. Now, it is a part of the most important process for the country, the EU integration that started in 2012, and is still ongoing. However, this process, as in other Western Balkans countries, is going slow, and the existing obstacles that the country is facing for years are persisting, such as dominance of major political parties, nepotism, corruption, slow reforms in all segments of society, all of which remain significant issues. This has been confirmed in the latest EU country progress reports that highlight political instability and lack of effective governance (European Commission, 2023d). Furthermore, Montenegro's economic development was strong but faced structural challenges, with a need for better fiscal management and market competitiveness.

The small size economy in 2021 mainly relies on the service sector (70%) and particularly on revenues from the growing tourism industry, with the industrial sector having limited capacities (13.5%), agriculture 9.1%, and construction (7.3%) (European Union, 2022).

The country has shown significant economic growth and poverty reduction between 2001 and 2008, which came because of a significant increase in real estate development, particularly Russian investors, buying and investing in properties on the coast. All these positive trends affected the Gross Domestic Product (GDP), which in 2023 was estimated at 6.81 billion euros, reflecting a GDP per capita of 11,037.15 euros. The poverty rate was projected at 9% (World Bank Group, 2024a), while the unemployment rate stood at 13.1% for the same year (World Bank Group, 2024b). The data indicates that the large part of the population is experiencing economic challenges, with unemployment levels remaining relatively high.

Overview of the Cultural and Creative Sector in Montenegro

Montenegro's current approach for developing the CCI sector is influenced by previous research, strategic documents, such as the National Strategy for Sustainable Development (2016), the Creative Montenegro Programme 2017–2020, the detailed mapping of CCI assets conducted in 2018, and later the Guidelines for the Development of CCI in Montenegro in 2019 (Ministry of Culture and Media, 2023, Institute for Entrepreneurship and Economic Development, 2020). These documents helped to identify the strengths, challenges, and opportunities within the sector.

Currently, the main directions of the existing National Strategy 2023–2027 focus on supporting creative individuals and businesses, helping them to strengthen economically and giving Montenegro a reputation as a place where cultural innovation will be produced (Ministry of Culture and Media, 2023). The Ministry sees creative work not only as an artistic expression but also as something with real economic value. A significant part of this strategy is the creation of creative hubs in the cities of Kotor, Bar, and Šavnik. These hubs are designed as places where artists and other creatives can come together, exchange ideas, and work on interdisciplinary projects. In addition to serving as collaborative spaces, these hubs are also intended to attract digital nomads – people who can work from anywhere – to live and work in Montenegro. The hope is that digital nomads will bring fresh energy and perspectives, helping these creative hubs become financially self-sustaining and keeping them buzzing with activity.

Another important goal is to use modern digital tools to revive Montenegro's cultural heritage. By embracing technology, the Ministry aims to make historical sites and cultural stories more accessible and engaging, adding to their educational value, attracting more visitors and boosting the local economy. This approach recognises that preserving cultural heritage is not just about protecting history; it is also about finding new ways to share it with the world in an era where digital experiences are increasingly important.

All of the above mentioned strategies and ideas will all become relevant and significant if they could and would be implemented. Like other countries in the Balkans, Montenegro faces difficulties in implementing the policies.

However, despite the acknowledgement of the relevance and importance of CCI for their significant contributions to the national economy, as well as their role in fostering social cohesion, there is still a lack of explicit and effective governmental instruments. Montenegro, like other countries in the region, is struggling with major challenges in carrying out the proposed strategies (Forum of Adriatic and Ionian Cities, 2022).

Lack of political will, human capacities, skills, and knowledge in the field, as well as a lack of sustained financial resources for field development, and lack of relevant data and research are the main challenges for the CCI in Montenegro.

Economic Contribution of the CCI

Based on the latest available data, the CCI sector in Montenegro contributed 1.5% to the gross value added (GVA) of the national economy, amounting to approximately EUR 53 million in 2017 (Institute for Entrepreneurship and Economic Development, 2019). Comparative data indicates that while the absolute GVA of the CCI sector increases alongside economic growth, its proportional share within the overall economy remains unchanged (Institute for Entrepreneurship and Economic Development, 2019). According to the Central European and Baltic States Newsletter 2023 the CCI contribute 3.4% of the GDP in Montenegro (Poland, CEBS WIPO Coordinator, 2023).

The 2018 CCI Mapping Report (Institute for Entrepreneurship and Economic Development, 2019) indicates that in 2017, Montenegro's Creative and Cultural Industries (CCI) sector comprised of 1,864 business entities, accounting for 3.5% of all registered enterprises. The data reveal a consistent upward trend in the number of CCI entities between 2014 and 2017, with growth predominantly generated by legal entities (See Figure 2.10).

As for the entities per sector, in percentage, as shown in Figure 2.11, the larger proportion of the employed are belonging to the advertising and marketing communications (integrated marketing communication) (16%), publishing and computer programs and games (each with 13%), music (12%), with the lowest number of employed in museums, libraries and heritage (2%).

Figure 2.10 Number of entities in CCI in Montenegro (2014–2017)

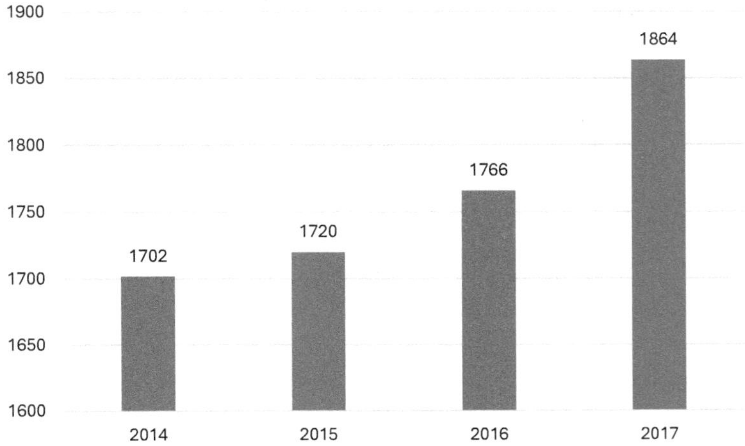

Figure 2.11 Number of entities (%) in CCI subsectors in Montenegro (2014–2017)

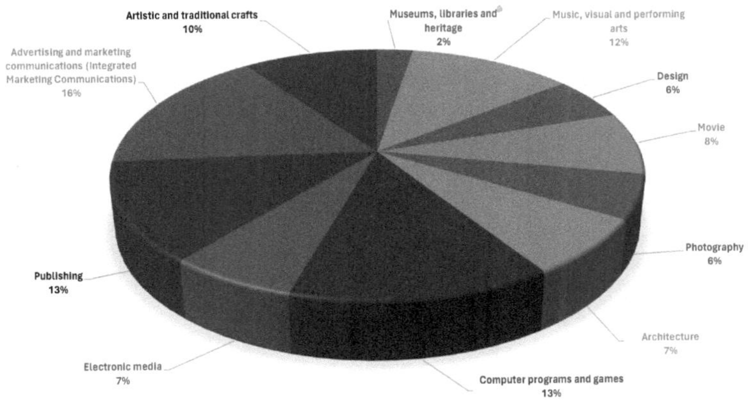

In terms of employment, the CCI sector engaged 4.4% of the country's workforce, with around 3,500 individuals working in creative and cultural jobs (Institute for Entrepreneurship and Economic Development, 2019). The same number of individuals are working in the CCI in 2020 according to Eurostat (2023).

Exports and International Presence

In 2022, the country recorded exports amounting to 51.5 billion euros, whereas imports were significantly higher, totalling 74.4 billion euros. This trade imbalance highlights a dependency on foreign goods and services, which may have implications for the country's external economic stability and currency valuation (World Bank Group, 2024a).

The CCI market in Montenegro is also reflected in its household consumption, with cultural consumption accounting for 2.3% of the total household spending in 2017. The sector generated a total revenue of EUR 127.2 million in 2017, showing its importance to the economy (Cuff and Zečević, 2022). However, exports from the CCI accounted for only 1.7% of total exports of services (Institute for Entrepreneurship and Economic Development, 2019).

Spotlight on Montenegro's Leading Creative Industries

Film and Cinema

The Film Centre of Montenegro is one of the most important institutions in the industry that supports and promotes national cinematography. Operating under the Law on Cinematography, this public institution is responsible for regulating, financing, and promoting film activities in the country and bringing the country cinematography on the European map (Film Centre of Montenegro, 2019). More info about this institution is given in Chapter 4.

Events such as Podgorica Film Festival are strengthening the film industry, with the possibility to promote and also build international relations and opportunities for young filmmakers to showcase their work.

The number of cinemas in Montenegro is very small, with only 11 in 2022, with a total of 240,484 visitors recorded in 2022 (Statistical Office of Montenegro, 2024).

Art and Design

Key institutions in this industry are the public institutions such as the National Museum of Montenegro and the Modern Art Gallery in Podgorica. Both are important generators in fostering artistic activities despite their challenges in relation with institutional support and employment structures. Art education, centred at the Faculty of Fine Arts in Cetinje, is another important pillar of this industry that supports emerging talents. However, in general, the sector faces challenges such as funding limitations and a small market. Opportunities for growth in this sector lie in tourism, digital platforms, and stronger ties to regional and European art scenes. As of 2021, Montenegro had 31 museums employing 383 people, reflecting the importance of cultural institutions in preserving the nation's heritage and promoting the contemporary arts (Statistical Office of Montenegro, 2024).

Fashion

The relatively small size of Montenegro's fashion industry, and having in mind the very limited local market, made this industry challenging for fashion designers to prosper. However, the country is home to a selection of creative and talented designers who are gradually making their mark on the local and international fashion scenes. Several fashion distinguished designers shape Montenegro's creative scene, including Aleksandra Džaković, founder of the brand AKKA; and Nina Čelebić who promote contemporary aesthetics with Montenegrian traditional elements (BIG SEE, 2021; Čelebić, n.d.).

Music and Performing Arts

The music industry in Montenegro faces substantial challenges due to the limited institutional support, low prioritisation in national cultural policy, and a modest musical tradition. Despite these obstacles, institutions like the Montenegrin Symphony Orchestra have made important steps forward, including organising the International Music Festival A TEMPO (European Festivals Association, n.d.). However, the sector remains under-supported compared to other cultural fields, lacking essential infrastructure, such as a professional concert hall. As a result, many music graduates leave the country due to lack of opportunities, despite the solid education system. The Montenegrin Music Centre, founded in 2006, aims to address these gaps, though its impact remains limited (Operabase, n.d.).

The theatre sector in Montenegro remains predominantly influenced by traditional approaches, with limited engagement in interdisciplinary experimentation (Mrđenović, 2020). It is represented by only a few main institutions, such as the National Theatre in Podgorica and Zetski Dom Royal Theatre in Cetinje, with independent productions occurring sporadically. The most notable theatre festivals are the Kotor Festival of Theatre for Children and the Montenegrin Theatre Biennale. According Statistical Office of Montenegro (2023), there are six professional and three amateur theatres. Employment in professional theatres rose from 279 in 2019 to 439 in 2022, while amateur theatre employment declined sharply from 63 to 16 in the same period, reflecting challenges in sustaining non-professional theatre activities.

The dance field remains underdeveloped, with no professional ensembles or significant institutional support, causing many young dancers and ballet professionals to seek opportunities abroad.

Digital and Gaming

Montenegro's digital and gaming industry is rapidly evolving, positioning itself as a potential hub for gaming and sports in the Adriatic region. The recent Adria Gaming Conference highlighted the industry's significant prospects. Filip Šoć, president of the Electronic Sports Association of Montenegro, emphasised the need for supportive legal frameworks for digital nomads and improvements in infrastructure to fully capitalise the industry's potential (Vijesti, 2023). Overall, Montenegro's gaming sector is well positioned for expansion, with opportunities for job creation and innovation across various fields.

Conclusion

CCI in Montenegro, despite facing several structural and financial challenges, are gradually evolving as a significant sector with the strong potential to impact the country's socioeconomic development. The tourism sector is an asset to this growing tendency of the sector. However, the lack of comprehensive policy frameworks and the limited access to funding continue to hinder its full potential, and the lack of capacities are factors that influence the sector. To move forward, it is crucial to establish a more sustainable institutional support, create capacity building opportunities for all stakeholders, and support greater collaboration (national and international) with the aim of creating a sustainable and growing creative ecosystem.

North Macedonia

The Demographic and Socio-Political Context of North Macedonia

According to the 2021 census, North Macedonia had a population of 1,836,713. The country's ethnic composition includes 58.44% Macedonians, 24.3% Albanians, 3.86% Turks, 2.53% Roma, 1.30% Serbs, 0.87% Bosniaks, and 0.47% Vlachs (State Statistical Office of the Republic of North Macedonia, 2023).

According to its constitution, North Macedonia (See Figure 2.12) is a multicultural country, with a population of diverse ethnic and religious backgrounds and with complex relations. This complexity in interethnic relations is reflected in all layers of society, starting from governance, decision-making, and the implementation of any strategies, national and local. This is especially critical in the dynamics of relations between the Macedonian and Albanian political blocs.

For this country, as for others in the Western Balkans, the most important process of the transition period is EU integration. It became a candidate country in 2005, but on its path to full integration, it faces major obstacles, despite the accession to NATO in 2020. The first obstacle came from the neighbouring Greece, which has been problematic over the country's name, culminating

Figure 2.12 Map of North Macedonia

Source: Google Maps. Screenshot was taken from Google map from [https://maps.app.goo.gl/YHb3TbjjMEeCnQzw7]

in a veto that has significantly delayed Macedonia's integration progress in the EU. The second major obstacle, which is still ongoing, comes from Bulgaria, which is also blocking the country's accession to the EU, citing unresolved historical disputes and the Macedonian language as the main reasons for the blockade (Simjanovska, 2022). These external challenges, together with internal interethnic tensions, have led to political polarisation and stagnation. Once a leading nation in the region, especially after the conflicts in former Yugoslavia, North Macedonia's development is currently stagnating, showing serious signs of regression. The European Commission report (2023c) highlights these setbacks, especially in the rule of law and the fight against corruption. In addition, the report points to slow reforms in public administration, ongoing issues with freedom of expression, and concerns about the effectiveness of judicial and anti-corruption measures.

Economically, North Macedonia is in a similar situation to other Western Balkan countries and is in the middle-income class. In 2023, the Gross Domestic Product (GDP) was €12.89 billion, with a GDP per capita of €7,033.85 (World Bank Group, 2024a). The distribution of economic activity by sector in 2022 shows a dominance of the services sector (58.8% of GDP), followed by the industrial sector with 22.9%, while agriculture is with 8.12% of the total economic output. These figures illustrate the country's orientation towards a service-dominated economy, with notable, even though smaller contributions from industry and agriculture.

The unemployment rate in North Macedonia, in 2022, was 14.40% (State Statistical Office of the Republic of North Macedonia, 2023), while the poverty rate was recorded at 14.43% for the same year (Macrotrends, n.d.).

The allocation of the state budget to culture fluctuated over the four years between 2018 and 2021, falling from 1.75% in 2018 to 1.23% in 2021 (Simjanovska, 2022).

Overview of the Cultural and Creative Sector in North Macedonia

The Ministry of Culture, which serves as the main authority for managing and guiding the development of the cultural sector, lack a well-defined or cohesive policy framework for the CCI (Simjanovska, 2022). Additionally, the CCI sector itself has not been explicitly defined. While the government bodies have acknowledged, at least on declarative level, the sector's potential for growth and its capacity to positively impact the national economy, no specific policies or instruments have been introduced to support it. Moreover, there is a significant gap in the collection and analysis of data related to this sector, including its classification, which directly affects the policy development process for the CCI field.

An exception within the broader sector is the film industry, which saw the establishment of an independent body in 2014 – the North Macedonia Film Agency – that provides stimulating financial instruments for its development (Simjanovska, 2022).

Despite the British Council's initial efforts to highlight the importance of the creative industries in North Macedonia through a 2009 sectoral mapping (British Council, 2010), the lack of subsequent dialogue or comprehensive strategies, aside from the Ministry of Culture's modest financial support for 72 projects totalling €48,000 (Simjanovska, 2022), reflects the decision-makers' insufficient awareness and capacity to address the sector's needs.

Economic Contribution of the CCI

The classification and measurement of the CCI in North Macedonia are complex and challenging due to their interconnection with other sectors and the multidimensional nature of culture. Variations in definitions, understandings, and data collection methodologies – such as those between Eurostat and Makstat – lead to different classifications across statistical domains, with distinct methods for cultural employment, trade, and participation statistics. In addition, much of the data is missing, particularly for the period after 2020. These factors make the data collection and analyses process particularly challenging.

According to the Regional Cooperation Council (2022), cultural enterprises in North Macedonia contributed €86 million in value added at factor cost, representing 2.3% of the total value added within the non-financial business economy, with a total turnover of €213 million, or 1.2% of that economy. However, Simjanovska (2022) highlights that GDP data for the CCI lack key elements for creating relevant cultural statistics. Despite this limitation, data covering sectors such as information and communication (J), professional and scientific activities (M), and arts and entertainment and recreation (R), indicate that their share of the total GDP grew from 3.75% in 2017 to 4.53% in 2020 (See Figure 2.13).

Based on the available data for 2020, the Information and Communication sector (J) has the largest portion of 52.88% of the total GDP, followed by the sector for Professional, Scientific, and Technical Activities (M) at 29.55%, while Arts, Entertainment, and Recreation (R) contributed 17.57% (See Figure 2.14) (State Statistical Office of North Macedonia, 2022).

In North Macedonia, the CCI sector has seen consistent growth in the number of entities from 3,050 in 2017 to 3,540 in 2020 (See Figure 2.15).

The available data shows growth in various CCI, with significant increases in areas such as the film industry, computer programming and gaming, while there are decreasing tendencies in publishing, photography, and some artistic crafts, particularly around 2020 (Simjanovska, 2022).

Figure 2.13 Participation of the selected CCI subsectors (J, M, and R) in GDP (%) in North Macedonia (2017–2020)

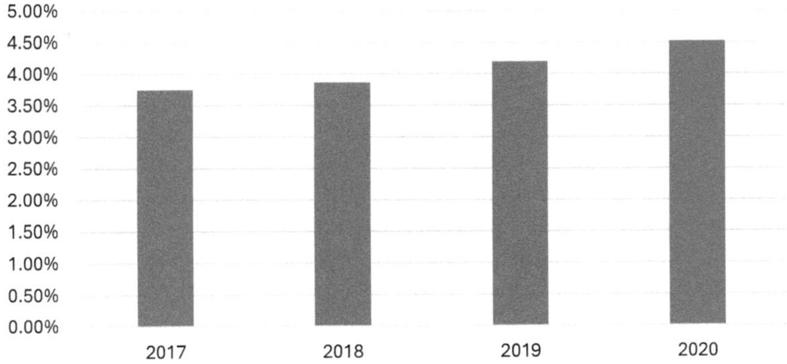

Figure 2.14 Participation of selected CCI in GDP (%) in North Macedonia (2017–2020)

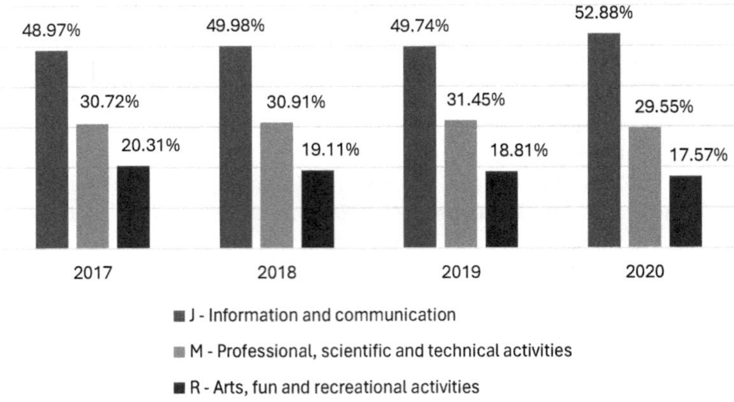

Figure 2.15 Total number of entities in CCI in North Macedonia (2017–2020)

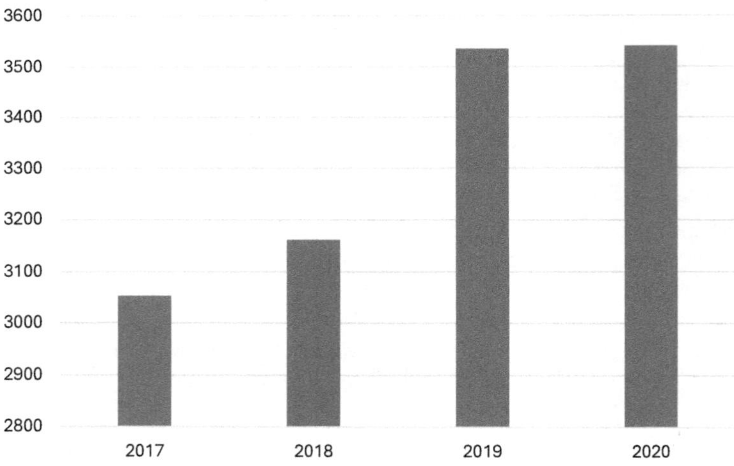

The cultural employment trends in North Macedonia over a four-year period, from 2017–2020, measured in thousands of persons, indicate fluctuations with a final upward momentum in 2020 to 25.2 thousand, with highlighting a growth trajectory for cultural employment by the end of the period and, in particularly, with the rise of the gaming industry (See Figure 2.16).

Figure 2.16 Cultural employment (in number, thousand persons) in North Macedonia (2017–2020)

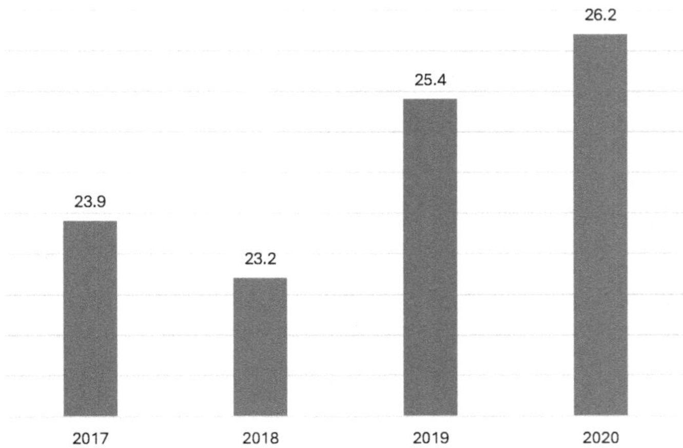

Export and International Presence

Available data for trade in cultural goods between North Macedonia and the world from 2017 to 2020, measured in thousands of euros, shows that North Macedonia consistently imported far more cultural goods than it exported, with a widening trade deficit in cultural goods, particularly as both exports and imports recorded a reduction by 2020, likely impacted by broader global factors such as the COVID-19 pandemic, conflicts, etc. In 2020, the import of cultural goods achieved EUR 19.646 thousand and the export only EUR 2.036 thousand (See Figure 2.17).

Figure 2.17 Trade in cultural goods in North Macedonia with all countries in the world (in thousand euros) (2017–2020)

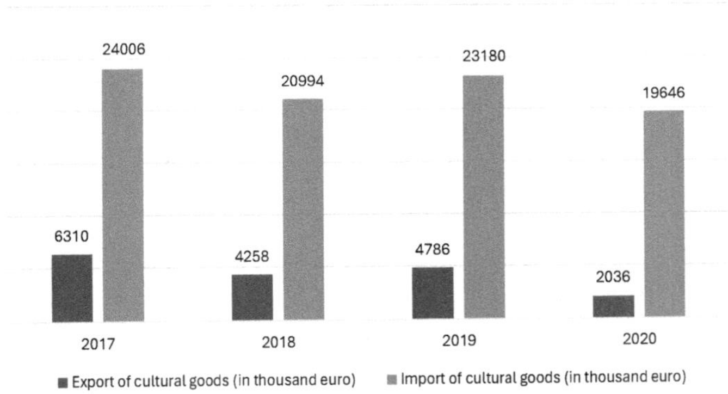

Spotlight on North Macedonia's Leading Creative Industries

Film and Cinema

According to the North Macedonia's Film Agency, in 2023, a total of 24 films were produced with an investment of €1,372,357, illustrating the continued commitment to developing local cinematic talent and production (North Macedonia's Film Agency, n.d.). The annual budget of the Film Agency fluctuates between €2 million and €6 million, in the last five years, reflecting both the scope of projects undertaken and the broader strategic initiatives aimed at elevating North Macedonian film on the global stage (North Macedonia Film Agency, n.d.; Simjanovska, 2022).

The film industry in North Macedonia has developed significantly in the past 30 years. The critical point in this upward line was when Milcho Manchevski, one of our most well-known filmmakers, won the Golden Lion at the Venice Film Festival in 1994. He attracted international attention and consequently, many international co-productions started to emerge, and many filmmakers had a chance to work on relevant film productions. Later, the filmmaker Teona Strugar Mitevska, along with Tamara Kotevska and Ljubomir Stefanov, marked a historic achievement for the country with their documentary Honeyland, which became the first Macedonian film to be nominated for an Academy Award in two categories: Best Documentary Feature and Best International Feature Film (*Academy of Motion Picture Arts and Sciences,* 2020). The contribution of the veteran Stole Popov is equally important for the cinematic legacy of North Macedonia, as his work has established the framework for the country's contemporary film industry.

Events, such as the Manaki Brothers International Film Festival in Bitola, that celebrates the art of cinematography and consistently attracts international attention positively influence the overall development of industry.

Despite these remarkable achievements, the North Macedonian film industry faces persistent challenges, including limited financial resources, insufficient infrastructure, nepotism in grant giving, and a relatively small domestic market. As a result, many filmmakers are forced to seek international co-productions and rely on external funding sources, such as Eurimages, to realise their projects.

In 2023, North Macedonia had 18 operational cinemas with 1,027 films shown, with 12,596 cinema performances and audience of 350,637, reflecting that films and cinema culture are still popular even though the local market is small.

Art and Design

The Art and Design in North Macedonia is with a relatively small size. The Museum of Contemporary Art in Skopje is one of the central institutions supporting modern and contemporary artists, both Macedonian and international. Several notable contemporary artists have emerged from North Macedonia, such as: Petar Hadzi Boshkov, Jordan and Iskra Grabul, Bedi Ibrahim, Iskra Dimitrova, Zhaneta Vangeli, Aco Stankovski, Jovan Shumkovski, Jane Chalovski, etc.

According to the State Statistical Office of North Macedonia (2022), 554 fine art exhibitions and 8 fine art colonies were organised in 2023, with 184,156 museum visitors recorded in 2021. Of the 25 museums, 16 are national, 8 are local, and 1 is private.

The design industry and particularly the graphic design in North Macedonia is growing, with numerous agencies and freelance designers operating in both local and international markets. Events such as the Skopje Design Week provide a platform for showcasing the latest in design trends.

Fashion

Fashion is another growing field, with Macedonian designers making their mark at home and abroad. Designers like Lidija Georgieva, Marjan Pejovski, Aleksandar Noshpal, Nikola Eftimov, Jovana Filkoska, and Elena Luka have gained attention for their creative practices. The country's fashion scene continues to grow, supported by events like Skopje Fashion Weekend. A new generation of North Macedonian designers is emerging, focusing on sustainability and environmentally conscious fashion. Brands like Bastet Noir, led by Daniela Milosheska, are pioneering zero-waste practices by repurposing discarded materials and employing single mothers as seamstresses. Other designers, such as Rosica Mrsik, are also producing sustainable collections using organic materials, although they face challenges due to the lack of public support, limited access to eco-friendly raw materials, and insufficient government support. These designers are working to align their practices with global trends, despite the difficulties in operating within North Macedonia's fashion industry (Kutuk, 2022).

Music and Performing Arts

North Macedonia's music industry, though modest, is working to keep up with the global trends like the rise of streaming. However, many musicians and cultural workers have struggled with the digital shift, particularly in mastering skills like digital marketing and content distribution. Copyright and intellectual property enforcement remains weak despite existing laws, and outdated systems for managing music genres have opened the door to manipulation and corruption. The industry also faces minimal regulation, leading many to operate in a legal grey area and rely on cash payments for work (Simjanovska, 2022).

Digital and Gaming

North Macedonia's game industry is developing rapidly and is among the fastest-growing sectors in the country's creative industries. Nevertheless, the government continues to neglect its economic and global importance. Successful examples, such as the indie game studio Furious Avocado, face numerous obstacles, including shortage of skilled personnel, outdated formal education or training programmes, and bureaucratic obstacles related to company registration and professional classification (Simjanovska, 2022).

The British Council's 2022 report on the gaming industry in North Macedonia highlights significant limitations in the way this industry sector is represented within the current Standard Industrial Classification (SIC) codes in the National Classification of Economic Activities (British Council, 2022). This makes it challenging to access relevant data through official sources such as the Central Registry of Business Entities and the State Statistical Office. Additionally, while new occupations are emerging within the GD industry, many are not yet incorporated into the National Classification of Occupations (SOC). Even for those that are included, official statistical information at the 4-digit code level remains unavailable.

Conclusion

The country's stagnation in nearly all societal segments, within its current political and economic context, negatively impacts the CCI sector. Despite the existing potential that the CCI in North Macedonia show, they face significant challenges. Political influence, corruption, nepotism, dysfunction of copyright low, ineffective administration, weak regulatory mechanisms, lack of quality education and skilled workforce in the cultural field, and un underdeveloped market are issues that impede the development of the sector (Simjanovska, 2022). However, the CCI sector's adaptability and willingness of individuals to engage in reform initiatives signal a promising future for its sustainable growth and international integration.

Serbia

The Demographic and Socio-Political Context of Serbia

The demographic map in Serbia in 2021 shows that the total number of inhabitants stood at 6,647,003 (Statistical Office of the Republic of Serbia, 2022). The demographic composition of Serbia comprised of 83.3% Serbs, 3.5% Hungarians, 2.1% Roma, 2% Bosnians, and approximately 5% smaller groups including Croats, Slovaks, Montenegrins, Vlachs, Romanians, Yugoslavs, and Macedonians, among others (European Commission, 2023a).

Serbia (See Figure 2.18), as other countries in the Western Balkans with turbulent past, struggled in the 1990s with the Miloshevic regime, a federation with Montenegro at that time, followed by obtaining a status of an EU candidate country since 2012 under a long-lasting populist government led by Aleksandar Vucic, with a significant political concern about the status of Kosovo and with a military neutral policy.

The issue with Kosovo is still an unsolved and a concerning issue, particularly for the stability of the country and the region. Although Serbia continues to regard Kosovo as an integral part of its national territory, a significant portion of the international community recognises Kosovo as a sovereign state. Nevertheless, several European Union member states, such as Spain and Cyprus, have not extended official recognition of its independence. The EU report on Serbia 2023 also puts doubt on Serbia's relations with the Russian Federation, particularly after the conflict with Ukraine (European

Figure 2.18 Map of Serbia

Source: Google Maps. Screenshot was taken from Google map from [https://maps.app.goo.gl/N4fP8t9MgEyDYbqe7]

Commission, 2023b). According to the same report, Serbia is not harmonised with the EU's restrictive policy towards the Russian Federation, nor does it align with most statements made by the EU High Representatives on this matter. Moreover, the same report indicates that the public administration reform in 2023 has seen only moderate advancement, while progress in the areas such as freedom of expression, corruption, and tackling organised crime remains limited (European Commission, 2023b). Despite these critical points, the official policy of Serbia confirms its orientation towards EU integration.

Serbia's economy is driven by a combination of the agriculture sector, which is a crucial contributor, and industrial manufacturing, including automotive, equipment, and chemical sectors. In addition, the fast-growing service industry, particularly in the field of information and communication technology (ICT), has an important impact. According to the World Bank (2024b), Serbia's Gross Domestic Product (GDP) was €68 billion in April 2024, with a GDP per capita of €10,140, suggesting that the country's economic situation has been steadily improving. The poverty rate in 2023 is 7.1%, indicating that the economic expansion has reduced socioeconomic disparities and improved the living standards (World Bank, 2024b).

Overview of the Cultural and Creative Sector in Serbia

Despite the lack of a coherent and consistent cultural policy that regulates the development of CCI within the Ministry of Culture, the Government of the Republic of Serbia has recognised the potential of CCI and has initiated several actions for its development. "The future is in creation, creativity, and the human mind" is a statement coming from the Prime Minister of the Republic of Serbia, Ana Brnabic. In regard to this statement, the same Prime Minister has initiated the Council for Creative Industries, whose role is to advise the prime minister's team and support the making of informed decisions that guide the sector's development in the most efficient ways. The other government initiative is "Serbia Creates," a national platform with an intersectoral approach whose main aim is to promote Serbia globally in the fields of CCI, innovation, and creative economies (Serbia Creates, n.d.-b).

In addition, the Association for Creative Industry of the Serbian Chamber of Commerce was formed, and it became an important stakeholder in conducting research and collecting data in the CCI sector, which in turn influences the legislative framework and creates a stimulating setting.

In 2019, the Sector for Development, International Cooperation, and Promotion of Digital, Innovative, and Creative Activities was established. This governmental body is responsible for formulating policy proposals related to digital and creative activities, coordinating international cooperation, and promoting global business practices (Cuff & Zečević, 2022).

Through these initiatives, the creative industries in Serbia have been gaining increasing recognition for their contribution to the country's economy, culture, and global presence. Yet, there is a lack of clear synergy among these initiatives and a lack of coherent government policy in regard to the development of CCI.

Economic Contribution of the CCI

Over the past decade, the CCI's impact on the national economy has ranged from 3.4% to 7.4%, depending on whether a broader or narrower definition of the industry is used (Cuff & Zečević, 2022).

In Serbia, as in many other countries, the distinction between the narrow and broader understanding of creative industries revolves around the range of activities included in the sector, based on the definitions and classifications used. University of Belgrade, Faculty of Economics (2022) states that several research studies in Serbia also use the narrow approach, which is based on the UK DCMS model. This model defines 30 key activities within the creative industries, organised into nine categories, while the broader definition extends to 52 activities (TERA Consultants, 2014).

According to the Chamber of Commerce and Industry of Serbia (n.d.), in 2022, the gross value added (GVA) generated by the creative industry reached 866.5 million EUR, equivalent to 1.8% of the country's total GVA, compared with 2021 when it reached 813.3 equivalent to 1.7% (See Figure 2.19).

According to the same source, the gross value added (total contribution 1.8%) of the CCI's in 2021 and its subsections is composed of 0.4% advertisement and market research, amounting to EUR 162.2 million, which is the largest portion, and 0.1% libraries, museums, and other activities, amounting to EUR 62.4 million, which is the smallest portion (See Figure 2.20).

Figure 2.19 Total GVA of creative industries in Serbia (2021)

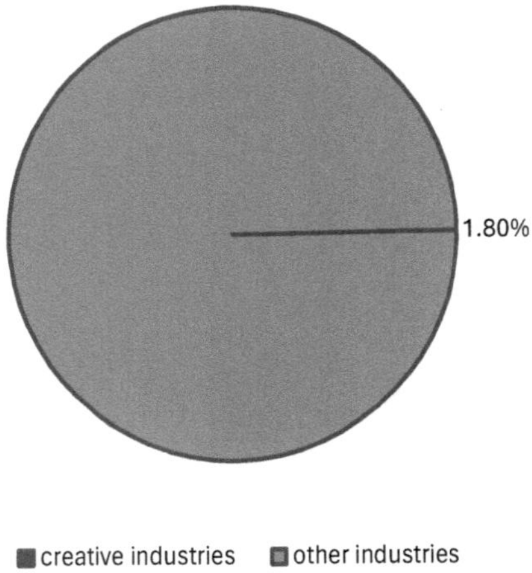

Figure 2.20 Share of GVA (%) per subsector in CCI in Serbia (2021)

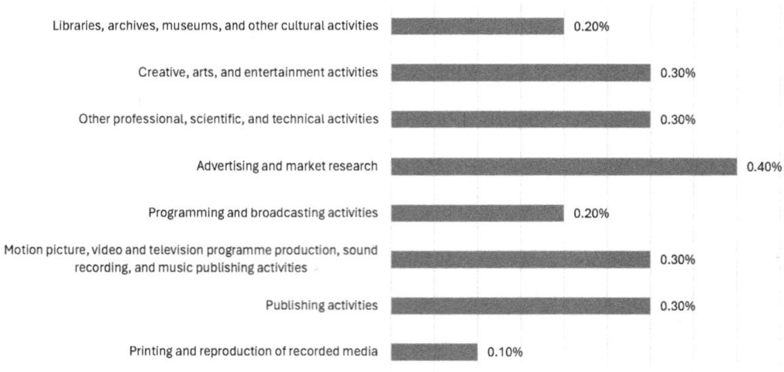

Market Trends and Employment

In 2022, Serbia's creative industry has 6,002 registered companies and 18,132 entrepreneurs actively contributing to the sector. In 2021, there were 5,867 companies within the sector, a 4% increase from 2020 (See Figure 2.21). This upward trend reflects the expanding influence of creative sectors, such as digitalisation and digital content creation, and particularly of the development of the gaming industry.

According to the Chamber of Commerce and Industry of Serbia (n.d.), the CCI sector employed 161,155 thousand workers in 2022, which represents

Figure 2.21 Number of Companies in the CCI sector in Serbia (2017–2022)

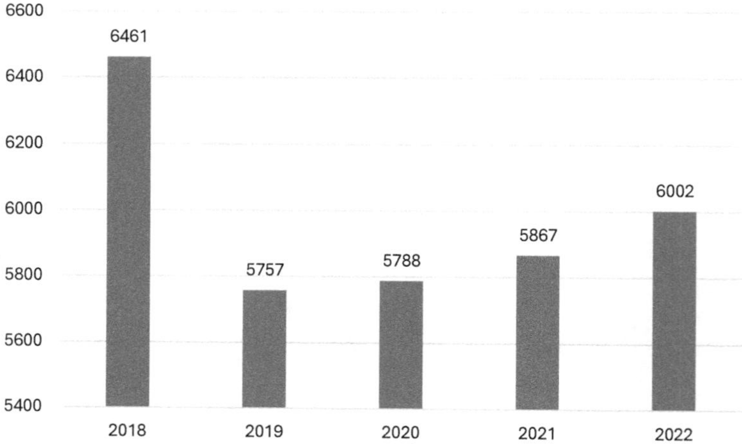

Figure 2.22 Number of employees in CCI in Serbia (2018–2022)

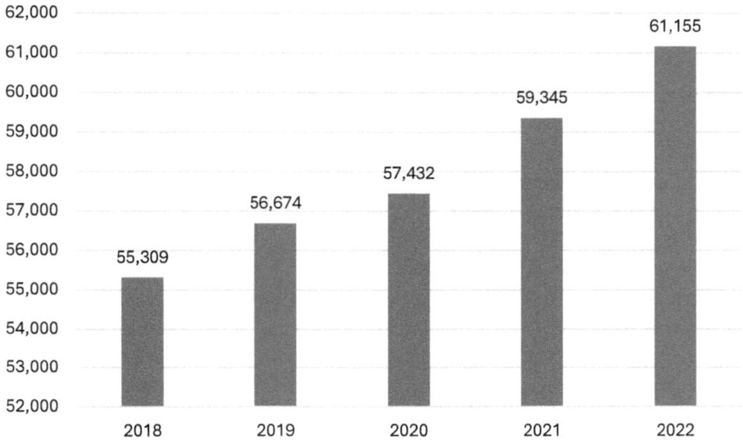

2.7% of the total employment in Serbia (See Figure 2.22). According to the same source, the largest employment sectors within the creative industries were arts and entertainment, with 10,152 thousand workers, and the lowest number are in the video, TV, sound, and music industries, accounting for 4.303.

Exports and International Presence

According to the data from the Statistical Office of the Republic of Serbia (2022) and the Chamber of Commerce and Industry of Serbia (2022), in 2022, the exports of audio and video records, musical instruments, photographic services, and other creative activities and services in Serbia totalled EUR 78.9 million. In 2022, the value of imports in these categories reached EUR 86.1 million. The foreign trade deficit in these goods amounted to EUR 7.2 million, with exports covering 91.6% of imports (Chamber of Commerce and Industry of Serbia, n.d.; Statistical Office of the Republic of Serbia, 2022).

Additionally, according to the Chamber of Commerce and Industry of Serbia (n.d.), the revenue from the export of audio, video, and related services in 2022 was EUR 147.8 million, resulting in a surplus of EUR 77.7 million (Chamber of Commerce and Industry of Serbia, n.d.; Statistical Office of the Republic of Serbia, 2022).

Spotlight on Serbia's Leading Creative Industries

Film and Cinema

The film industry is one of the rapid growing sectors in Serbia. The legacy of the industry relies on the well-known world filmmakers such as Dushan

Makavejev, Zhelimir Zhilnik, Srdjan Dragojevic, Goran Paskaljevic, Goran Markovic, Maja Milosh, Emir Kusturica, etc. The country's strategic orientation is to significantly increase investments in this industry, aided by attractive tax incentives. Recently, the country has gained recognition as a desirable film location, drawing numerous international projects and co-productions.

The film industry is managed by the Serbia Film Centre, a governmental body of national importance that provides professional support to filmmakers and film professionals with an annual budget (2021) of 2,046,811 EUR (Film Center Serbia, n.d.-b; Cuff & Zečević, 2022). According to the latest information of the Statistical Office of the Republic of Serbia (2022), there were a total of 34 film productions in 2021, compared to only 16 in 2017. According to the Film Centre Serbia (n.d.-a), there were 17 feature films supported in 2023, 14 feature documentaries, and 1 feature animated films. In addition, television production and film services in Serbia have undergone significant growth in recent years. The country is increasingly emerging as a regional hub for international co-productions and film service collaborations, attracting companies from the USA, the United Kingdom, and EU member states. This development is largely driven by Serbia's skilled talent pool, cost-effective production environment, and well-developed filming infrastructure.

Serbia has a total of 97 cinemas and has shown 147.193 films in 2022. In the same year, there were 2,758,000 visitors (Statistical Office of the Republic of Serbia, 2022).

Art and Design

A well-known, and for some arts professionals controversial, artist from Serbia, Marina Abramović, once stated, "I realise the power of art that does not hang on the walls of galleries" (BBC StoryWorks, n.d.). This statement looks relevant for Serbia and emphasises how important art is in all its manifestations. Serbia is a country with a growing creative sector that offers various art forms, starting from contemporary, urban, modern, street, and traditional art, with a particular emphasis on visual arts, architecture, and design. The Statistical Office of the Republic of Serbia (2022) notes that 150 museums and numerous galleries enrich the country's cultural landscape with a multitude of art collections and exhibitions. These institutions not only produce, curate, and promote exhibitions, but they are also good promoters and supporters of the export of arts goods, educational initiatives, and community-based projects. Some of the leading organisations in this sector include Belgrade Art Studio, Remont Gallery, Museum of Modern Art, and Cultural Centre of Belgrade.

Music and Performing Arts

Serbia's music industry has experienced growth in recent years. It's contribution to the economy is approximately 14,959 employees in 2022 or 0.66% of Serbia's total employment (Government of the Republic of Serbia (2024) and University of Belgrade, Faculty of Economics (2024). It is important to mention that most of these numbers refer to part-time jobs or temporary contracts. Only 33% of the total workforce in this industry is employed full-time. One of the challenges in this subsector for all music professionals is finding permanent jobs (Government of the Republic of Serbia (2024) and University of Belgrade, Faculty of Economics (2024).

The other performing arts fields, such as theatre, dance, and experimental art, contribute significantly to Serbia's CCI. According to the Statistical Office of the Republic of Serbia (2022), there are 97 active theatres with 5491 performances in 2022, of which 37 are professional theatres, 47 are amateur theatres, and 13 are children's theatres. This subsector in Serbia is vibrant, mainly maintained by public organisations, but also private theatres and other forms of independent art organisations.

The most prominent organisations in this field in Serbia are Dom Omladine, Belgrade Drama Theatre, Yugoslav Drama Theatre, Atelje 212, Sterijino Pozorje, Dah Theatre, BAZAART, Reflektor, Stanica, Cirkusfera, etc. The publicly supported performing arts organisations have a privileged position due to their publicly secured subsidies and due to having their own space. Given the underdeveloped market and economy, as well as the theatres' non-advantageous position in terms of government support of any kind, a significant degree of these organisations is withholding from the field. In addition to the performing arts organisation, there are a few festivals that play an enormous role in the field. One of the most remarkable is the Belgrade International Theatre Festival (BITEF), which plays a crucial role in showcasing contemporary performing arts (Knežević, 2022).

Fashion

The fashion industry in Serbia is steadily gaining recognition, supported by initiatives such as Belgrade Fashion Week, which highlight the creativity of both established and emerging designers. While the sector continues to evolve, notable individuals such as Roksanda Ilinčić, a London-based designer born and educated in Serbia, and internationally recognised costume designer Bojana Nikitović exemplify the global reach and talent emerging from the country (Nikitović, n.d.).

Digital and Gaming

The gaming sector in Serbia is rapidly accelerating economic and technological advancement, as evidenced by its rapid global growth. With an annual revenue of EUR 120 million and a remarkable yearly growth rate of 20%, the sector is not only vibrant, but it is also playing a more prominent role in Serbia's broader technological ecosystem (Serbia Creates, n.d.-b). Of particular significance is the purchase of three highly prosperous gaming enterprises in Serbia by foreign investors over the last two years, which serves as evidence of the global acknowledgement of Serbia's exceptional skills and future prospects. The acquisitions have facilitated the entry of major multinational companies such as Nordeus, Epic Games, Playrix, and Take-Two Interactive Software into the Serbian industry, greatly improving its global prominence.

Furthermore, the gaming sector in Serbia is characterised by its inclusiveness, particularly in relation to gender diversity. These findings highlight the forward-thinking character of the business and indicate the wider societal changes towards more gender balanced society. Serbia's creative industries, featuring gaming as a leading sector, remain a crucial driver of the country's economic vitality and globally recognised innovation.

Conclusion

Serbia's CCI are key in shaping the cultural identity, global reputation, and also influencing the economy. Despite facing various challenges in recent years, the sector continues to drive growth, innovation, and job creation. Sectors such as film and gaming industry are the leading ones in CCI on local and regional level. By continuing to invest in a more systematic way and in areas such as gaming, film, performing arts, music and fashion, Serbia is well positioned to strengthen its role as a leading creative hub in the Balkans.

References

Academy of Motion Picture Arts and Sciences. (2002). *The 74th academy awards (2002) nominees and winners*. https://www.oscars.org/oscars/ceremonies/2002

Academy of Motion Picture Arts and Sciences. (2020). *The 92nd academy awards (2020) nominees and winners*. https://www.oscars.org/oscars/ceremonies/2020

Academy of Motion Picture Arts and Sciences. (2021). *The 93rd academy awards (2021) nominees and winners*. https://www.oscars.org/oscars/ceremonies/2021

Adorno, T. W., & Horkheimer, M. (1944). *Dialectic of enlightenment*. Stanford University Press.

Adorno, T. W., & Horkheimer, M. (1979). The cultural industry: Enlightenment as mass deception. In J. Curran, M. Gurevich, & J. Woollacott (Eds.), *Mass communication and society* (pp. 349–384). Verso.

Agency for Statistics of Bosnia and Herzegovina. (2023). *Kultura i umjetnost 2022* [Culture and art 2022]. https://bhas.gov.ba/data/Publikacije/Bilteni/2023/CUL_00_2022_TB_1_BS.pdf

Albanian National Center of Cinematography. (n.d.). *About us*. Qendra Kombëtare e Kinematografisë. Retrieved July 4, 2025, from https://qkk.al/

Albdesign. (n.d.). *Albdesign*. http://albdesign.al/

All Correct Games. (n.d.). *The Balkan gaming market*. https://allcorrectgames.com/insights/the-balkan-gaming-market/

Art Kontakt. (n.d.). *About art Kontakt*. https://www.artkontakt.al/en/about/

Asocijacija arhitekata u Bosni i Hercegovini. (n.d.). *AABH Creative Hub: Ko su naši korisnici?* [AABH creative hub: Who are our users?]. https://aabh.ba/aabh-creative-hub-ko-su-nasi-korisnici/

Australia. Department of Communications and the Arts. (1994). *Creative nation: Commonwealth cultural policy* (102 pp.). Canberra: Department of Communications and the Arts.

Baker, C. (2007). The concept of turbofolk in Croatia: Inclusion/exclusion in the construction of national musical identity. In C. J. Gerry, B. Madaj, L. Mellish, & J. Nahodilová (Eds.), *Nation in formation: Inclusion and exclusion in Central & Eastern Europe* (pp. 139–158). UCL School of Slavonic and East European Studies.

Barnett, G. A., & Lee, M. (2002). Issues in intercultural communication research. In W. B. Gudykunst & B. Mody (Eds.), *Handbook of international and intercultural communication* (2nd ed., pp. 275–290). Sage.

BBC StoryWorks. (n.d.). *Experience Serbia: Art and culture*. https://www.bbc.com/storyworks/travel/experience-serbia/art-and-culture

Begić, A. (Director & Writer). (2008). *Snow* [Film]. Mamafilm; Rohfilm GmbH; Les Films de l'Après-midi; Documentary & Experimental Film Center; with support from Pyramide International.

Begić, A. (Director & Writer). (2012). *Children of Sarajevo* [Film]. Bosnia and Herzegovina; Germany; France; Turkey: Film House Sarajevo; Rohfilm GmbH; Kaplan Film; Les Films de l'Après-midi.

Bianchini, F., & Parkinson, M. (Eds.). (1993). *Cultural policy and urban regeneration: The West European experience*. Manchester University Press.

BIG SEE. (2021). *Aleksandra Džaković /Akka/Archaic future*. https://bigsee.eu/aleksandra-dzakovic-akka-archaic-future/

Bit Alliance. (n.d.-a). *About bit alliance*. https://bit-alliance.ba/about/

Bit Alliance. (n.d.-b). *United to develop more: Leading association of IT companies in B&H*. https://bit-alliance.ba/

Breznica, R. K., Luzha, B., Gagica-Rexhepi, F., & Rexhepi, B. R. (2024). An analysis of the economic impact potential of the art music scene in Kosovo: Is it a burden or an additional value for society? *International Journal of Religion*, *5*(5), 460–474. https://doi.org/10.61707/0w0at813

British Council. (2010). *Creative industries mapping in the Republic of Macedonia*. British Council. https://oer.makingprojects.org/wp-content/uploads/2018/10/Skopje/Unit3/UNIT3_1_learning_material_mapping_of_the_creative_industries_in_Macedonia.pdf

British Council. (2022). *Mapping the game development industry in Macedonia*. British Council. https://magda.org.mk/wp-content/uploads/2022/12/mapping_the_game_development_industry_in_macedonia-en.pdf

Čelebić, N. (n.d.). *Nina Čelebić – fashion designer*. https://www.linkedin.com/in/nina-celebic-06a93088

Chamber of Commerce and Industry of Serbia. (2022). *Annual bulletin 2022: Association of creative industry*. Chamber of Commerce and Industry of Serbia. https://api.pks.rs/storage/assets/Association%20of%20Creative%20Industry,%202022.pdf

Chamber of Commerce and Industry of Serbia. (n.d.). *Association of creative industry*. Retrieved September 22, 2024, from https://en.pks.rs/industry-associations/association-2

Council of the European Union. (2015). *Stabilisation and association agreement (SAA) between the European Union and Kosovo signed* [Press release]. https://www.consilium.europa.eu/en/press/press-releases/2015/10/27/kosovo-eu-stabilisation-association-agreement/pdf

Cuff, M., & Zečević, I. (2022). *Mapping of the creative industries in the Western Balkans*. Regional Cooperation Council. https://www.rcc.int/pubs/137/mapping-of-the-creative-industries-in-the-western-balkans

Cvetičanin, P. (2023). *Nerazumevanje stanja kulture u Srbiji danas* [Misunderstanding the state of culture in Serbia today]. SEEcult.org. https://www.seecult.org/cveticanin-nerazumevanje-stanja-kulture-u-srbiji-danas/

Cvetičanin, P., Pereira, L. P., Petrić, M., Tomić-Koludrović, I., Lebaron, F., & Zdravković, Ž. (2024). Cultural practices and socio-digital inequalities in Europe: Towards a unified research framework in cultural participation studies. *Cultural Sociology*, *0*(0). https://doi.org/10.1177/17499755231222520

Delta Print Studio. (n.d.). *Delta print studio*. https://deltaprintstudio.weebly.com/

Department for Digital, Culture, Media & Sport. (1998). *Creative industries mapping documents 1998*. GOV.UK. https://www.gov.uk/government/publications/creative-industries-mapping-documents-1998

Dragicevic Sesic, M. (n.d.). *Za kulturu, protiv kreativnih industrija* [For culture, against creative industries]. https://likumzg.wordpress.com/dr-milena-dragicevic-sesic/

Dragićević Šešić, M. (2011a). Cultural policies, identities and monument building in Southeastern Europe. In A. Milohnić & N. Švob-Đokić (Eds.), *Cultural identity politics in the (post)transitional societies* (pp. 31–46). Institute for International Relations.

European Commission. (2023a). *Serbia: Population demographic situation, languages, and religions*. Eurydice. https://eurydice.eacea.ec.europa.eu/national-education-systems/serbia/population-demographic-situation-languages-and-religions

European Commission. (2023b). *Serbia 2023 report*. https://www.mei.gov.rs/upload/documents/eu_dokumenta/godisnji_izvestaji_ek_o_napretku/ec_report_serbia_2023.pdf

European Commission. (2023c). *North Macedonia 2023 report (SWD(2023) 693 final)*. https://neighbourhood-enlargement.ec.europa.eu/system/files/2023-11/SWD_2023_693%20North%20Macedonia%20report.pdf

European Commission. (2023d). *Key findings of the 2023 report on Montenegro*. https://ec.europa.eu/commission/presscorner/detail/en/QANDA_23_5615

European Commission. (n.d.-a). *Albania: Country overview*. https://webgate.ec.europa.eu/isdb_results/factsheets/country/overview_albania_en.pdf

European Commission. (n.d.-b). *Albania: Enlargement policy*. https://neighbourhood-enlargement.ec.europa.eu/enlargement-policy/albania_en

European Commission. (n.d.-c). *Bosnia and Herzegovina: Enlargement policy*. https://neighbourhood-enlargement.ec.europa.eu/enlargement-policy/bosnia-and-herzegovina_en

European Commission. (n.d.-d). *Population: Demographic situation, languages and religion – Bosnia and Herzegovina*. https://eurydice.eacea.ec.europa.eu/national-education-systems/bosnia-and-herzegovina/population-demographic-situation-languages-and

European Festivals Association. (n.d.). *International music festival a TEMPO*. https://www.festivalfinder.eu/festivals/international-music-festival-a-tempo

European Theatre Convention. (n.d.). *National theatre of Albania*. https://www.europeantheatre.eu/member/national-theatre-of-albania

European Union. (2022). *Montenegro – country report 2022*. https://ec.europa.eu/eurostat/documents/4031688/14589427/KS-05-22-089-EN-N.pdf

Eurostat. (2023). *Culture statistics – cultural employment 2023* [Data file]. https://ec.europa.eu/eurostat/statistics-explained/images/c/c8/Culture_statistics_-_cultural_employment_2023.xlsx

Eurostat. (2024). *Key figures for candidate countries and potential candidates*. Retrieved August 8, 2024, from https://ec.europa.eu/eurostat/statistics-explained/index.php?title=Key_figures_for_candidate_countries_and_potential_candidates

Eurostat. (n.d.-a). *Cultural employment by sex*. https://ec.europa.eu/eurostat/databrowser/view/CULT_EMP_SEX/default/table?lang=en&category=cult.cult_emp

Eurostat. (n.d.-b). *Intra and extra-EU trade in cultural goods by product*. https://ec.europa.eu/eurostat/databrowser/view/CULT_TRD_PRD/default/table?lang=en&category=cult.cult_trd_go?lang=en&category=cult.cult_trd_go

Festival de Cannes. (n.d.-a). *Danis Tanović*. https://www.festival-cannes.com/en/p/danis-tanovic/

Festival de Cannes. (n.d.-b). *Djeca (children of Sarajevo)*. https://www.festival-cannes.com/en/f/djeca/

Festival de Cannes. (n.d.-c). *Miracle in Bosnia*. https://www.festival-cannes.com/en/

Film Center Serbia. (n.d.-a). *Film database*. https://www.fcs.rs/en/film-database/

Film Center Serbia. (n.d.-b). *About us*. https://www.fcs.rs/en/fcs/about-us/

Film Centre of Montenegro. (2019). *Zakon o kinematografiji-2015* [Law on cinematography-2015].https://fccg.me/wp-content/uploads/2019/04/2.-Zakon-o-kinematografiji.pdf

Flew, T. (2012). *The creative industries: Culture and policy*. SAGE Publications Ltd. https://doi.org/10.4135/9781446288412

Florida, R. (2002). *The rise of the creative class: And how it's transforming work, leisure, community, and everyday life*. Basic Books.

Florida, R. (2005). *The flight of the creative class: The new global competition for talent*. HarperBusiness.

Forum of Adriatic and Ionian Cities. (2022). *AI-NURECC PLUS conference: Development models for creative and cultural industries in the Adriatic-Ionian region*. https://www.faic.eu/en/ai-nurecc-plus-conference-development-models-for-creative-and-cultural-industries-in-the-adriatic-Ionian-region/

Galloway, S., & Dunlop, S. (2007). A critique of definitions of the cultural and creative industries in public policy. *International Journal of Cultural Policy*, *13*(1), 17–31. https://doi.org/10.1080/10286630701201657

GAP Institute for Advanced Studies. (2012). *The economic impact of DokuFest*. https://www.institutigap.org/news/140

Garnham, N. (1990). *Capitalism and communication*. Sage.
Government of Montenegro. (2016). *National strategy for sustainable development of Montenegro until 2030*.
Government of the Republic of Serbia. (2024, March 22). *Music industry in Serbia records 89 percent turnover growth*. https://www.srbija.gov.rs/vest/en/220782/music-industry-in-serbia-records-89-percent-turnover-growth.php
Grodach, C., Foster, N., & Murdoch, J. (2023). Cultural policy in post-industrial cities: Creative industries and inclusive development. *The British Journal of Sociology*, *74*(1), 49–70. https://doi.org/10.1111/1468-4446.12858
Guri, N. (2019). *Developing a gaming future*. Kosovo 2.0. https://kosovotwopointzero.com/en/developing-a-gaming-future/
Hancıgàz, E., & Hülür, H. (2024). The role of Turkish TV series in the formation of perception about Turkey and Turkish people: The cases of Bosnia and Herzegovina, Jordan and Kyrgyzstan. *Ege Akademik Bakış/Ege Academic Review*, *24*(2). https://doi.org/10.21121/eab.1391570
Hartley, J. (2021). *Advanced introduction to creative industries*. Edward Elgar Publishing.
Havoli, B., Fairburn, J., Pugh, G., Talam, E., Efendic, A., & Stojcic, N. (2023). *Promoting the creative sector in three deindustrialised economies: The United Kingdom; Bosnia and Herzegovina; and Croatia (project report)*. Staffordshire University. https://eprints.staffs.ac.uk/8013/
Hesmondhalgh, D. (2002). *The cultural industries*. Sage Publications.
Howkins, J. (2001). *The creative economy: How people make money from ideas*. Penguin.
Innovation Centre Banja Luka. (n.d.). *Innovation centre Banja Luka*. https://icbl.ba/
Institute for Entrepreneurship and Economic Development. (2019). *Mapping of cultural and creative industries in Montenegro: Assessment of the economic contribution of the cultural and creative industries*. https://kreativneindustrije.me/wp-content/uploads/2020/04/Mapping-of-Cultural-and-Creative-Industries-in-Montenegro.pdf
Institute for Entrepreneurship and Economic Development. (2020). *Results of the first call 'creative Montenegro: Identity, image, promotion 2017–2020'*. https://kreativneindustrije.me/en/results-of-the-first-call-creative-montenegro-identity-image-promotion-2017-2020/
Institute of Statistics of Albania. (2021). *Culture statistics 2021*. https://www.instat.gov.al/media/10161/culture-statistics-2021.pdf
Institute of Statistics of Albania. (2023). *Quarterly economic growth: First quarter, 2023*. https://www.instat.gov.al/media/11808/gdp-q1–2023.pdf
International Monetary Fund. (2023). *Republic of Kosovo: First reviews under the stand-by arrangement and the arrangement under the resilience and sustainability facility and request for modification of reform measure – press release; staff report; and statement by the executive director for Republic of Kosovo (IMF country report no. 23/372)*.
International Trade Administration. (2024). *Kosovo – country commercial guide: Market overview*. https://www.trade.gov/country-commercial-guides/kosovo-market-overview
Jovičić, S., & Mikić, H. (2006). *Kreativne industrije: Preporuke za razvoj kreativnih industrija u Srbiji* [Creative industries: Recommendations for

the development of creative industries in Serbia]. British Council Serbia and Montenegro.
Jović, D. (2009). *Yugoslavia: A state that withered away*. Purdue University Press.
Judah, T., & Vračić, A. (2019, May 2). *The Western Balkans' statistical black hole*. European Council on Foreign Relations. https://ecfr.eu/article/commentary_western_balkans_statistical_black_hole_eu_enlargement/
Kalender, A. (2014). Country report: Bosnia and Herzegovina. In V. Simjanovska, V. Ratzenböck, & A. Kalender (Eds.), *KULTURLOGUE: Evaluation of cultural policies and EU-funded programmes as promoters of cultural diversity and intercultural dialogue in the Balkans/Southeast Europe (SEE)* (pp. 20–34). Performing Arts Center Multimedia.
Knežević, J. (Ed.). (2022). *Mapping the performing arts in Serbia*. IETM – International Network for Contemporary Performing Arts. https://www.ietm.org/system/files/publications/V03_IETM_Belgrade%20Mapping.pdf
Kosova Cinematography Centre (KCC). (n.d.). *Title of the webpage or document*.
Kosovo Agency of Statistics. (2023). *Culture statistics, 2022*. https://ask.rks-gov.net/Releases/Details/7592
Kutuk, D. (2022). *How North Macedonia's fashion labels aim to reduce textile waste*. TRT World. https://www.trtworld.com/magazine/how-north-macedonia-s-fashion-labels-aim-to-reduce-textile-waste-57234
Kuzmanova, V. (2021). Gaming studio Nordeus acquired by take-two interactive in a huge exit for Serbia. *The Recursive*. https://therecursive.com/gaming-studio-nordeus-acquired-by-take-two-interactive-in-a-huge-exit-for-serbia/
La Biennale di Venezia. (2020). *Quo Vadis, Aida?* https://www.labiennale.org/en/cinema/2020/venezia-77-competition/quo-vadis-aida
Lukić, T., & Živković, J. (2017). Independent cultural scene and survival strategies in Serbia. In D. Radić & B. Vučetić (Eds.), *Cultural memory, politics and change* (pp. 85–101). University of Arts in Belgrade.
Luthar, B., & Pušnik, M. (Eds.). (2010). *Remembering utopia: The culture of everyday life in socialist Yugoslavia*. New Academia Publishing.
Macrotrends. (n.d.). *North Macedonia unemployment rate*. https://www.macrotrends.net/global-metrics/countries/MKD/north-macedonia/unemployment-rate
Manifesta 14. (n.d.). *Manifesta 14 Prishtina*. https://manifesta14.org/
Marku, A., & Teqja, E. A. (2024). The European integration process of Western Balkans, time for a new approach. *Journal of Educational and Social Research*, *14*(1). https://doi.org/10.36941/jesr-2024–0011
McGuigan, J. (1996). *Culture and the public sphere*. Routledge.
McGuigan, J. (2009). *Cool capitalism*. Pluto.
Mège, B. (1989). *The capitalization of cultural production*. International General.
MESS. (n.d.). *MESS: International theater festival Sarajevo*. https://mess.ba/
Mikić, H. (2013). *Kreativne industrije u BiH: Moguće perspektive razvoja* [Creative industries in Bosnia and Herzegovina: Possible development perspectives]. Centre for Policy and Governance. https://www.cpu.org.ba/media/19417/Prezentacija-Hristina-Mikic.pdf
Ministry of Culture and Media. (2023). *Nacionalni program razvoja kulture 2023–2027 [National cultural development program 2023–2027]*. Government of Montenegro.

Ministry of Economy, Culture, and Innovation. (2019). *National strategy for culture 2019–2025*. Republic of Albania. https://meki.gov.al/strategjia-kombetare-per-kulturen-2/

Mrđenović, M. (2020). Theatre in Montenegro: An unfinished cultural transition. *Critical Stages/Scènes critiques*, *21*. https://www.critical-stages.org/21/theatre-in-montenegro-an-unfinished-cultural-transition/

Mustafić, D., & Tanović, D. (Directors). (1995). *Miracle in Bosnia* [Documentary film]. Bosnia and Herzegovina: FAOS; co-produced by MFS EMMA (Letterboxd)

National Endowment for Science, Technology and the Arts. (2006). *Creating growth: How the UK can develop world-class creative businesses*. NESTA. https://media.nesta.org.uk/documents/creating_growth.pdf

National Gallery of Kosovo. (n.d.). *About us*. https://www.galeriakombetare-rks.com/en

Nikitović, B. (n.d.). *Bojana Nikitović – costume designer*. https://www.bojananikitovic.com/

North Macedonia Film Agency. (n.d.). *Финансирани филмски проекти* [Financed film projects]. https://filmfund.gov.mk/?page_id=1199

NSoft. (n.d.). *About us*. https://www.nsoft.com/about-us

Nurkovic, R. (2015). Contemporary development of creative industries in Bosnia and Herzegovina. *Quaestiones Geographicae*, *34*(2), 45–51. https://doi.org/10.1515/quageo-2015-0014

O'Connor, J. (2010). *The cultural and creative industries: A literature review* (2nd ed.). Creativity, Culture and Education.

ODA Theatre. (n.d.). *About us*. https://teatrioda.com/en/about-us/

OECD. (2024). *Western Balkans competitiveness outlook 2024: Regional profile*. OECD Publishing. https://www.oecd.org/content/dam/oecd/en/publications/reports/2024/06/western-balkans-competitiveness-outlook-2024-regional-profile_359dd5b9/170b0e53-en.pdf

Operabase. (n.d.). *Montenegrin music center*. https://www.operabase.com/montenegrin-music-center-o33676/about/en

Organisation for Economic Co-operation and Development [OECD]. (2022). *SME policy index: Western Balkans and Turkey 2022 – assessing the implementation of the small business act for Europe*. OECD Publishing. https://doi.org/10.1787/b47d1f50-en

Organization for Security and Co-Operation in Europe [OSCE]. (2014). *Community rights assessment report* (2nd ed.). https://www.osce.org/files/f/documents/e/0/126173.pdf

Petrović, T. (Ed.). (2014). *Mirroring Europe: Ideas of Europe and Europeanization in Balkan societies* (Vol. 13). Brill. https://brill.com/display/title/28948

Poland, CEBS WIPO Coordinator. (2023). *The power of Central European and Baltic States (CEBS): Creative industries* (No. 2). https://upv.gov.cz/files/uploads/PDF_Dokumenty/aktuality/Newsletter_2_2023.pdf

Primorac, J. (2006). *The position of cultural workers in creative industries: The south-eastern European perspective*. Institute for International Relations.

https://culturalfoundation.eu/wp-content/uploads/2021/02/CPRA_Cultural Workers.pdf

Primorac, J. (2014). The position and perspectives of cultural and creative industries in Southeastern Europe/Položaj i perspektive kulturnih i kreativnih industrija u Jugoistočnoj Europi. *Medijska istraživanja: Znanstveno-stručni časopis za novinarstvo i medije, 20*(1), 45–65.

ReDo Prishtina. (2024). *Edition 12: 4–6 October 2024, Prishtina, Kosovo*. https://redoprishtina.com/#information

Regional Cooperation Council. (2022). *Mapping of the creative industries in the Western Balkans*. Regional Cooperation Council. https://www.rcc.int/pubs/137/mapping-of-the-creative-industries-in-the-western-balkans

Ryan, B. (1992). *Making capital from culture: The corporate form of capitalist cultural production*. De Gruyter. https://doi.org/10.1515/9783110847185

Sabo, I. (2022). *The Serbian games association: From hero story to gaming ecosystem*. Swiss Entrepreneurship Program. https://swissep.org/our-impact/success-stories/the-serbian-games-association-from-hero-story-to-gaming-ecosystem

Sarajevo City of Film. (n.d.-a). *Sarajevo film fund*. https://sarajevocityoffilm.ba/sarajevo-film-fund/

Sarajevo City of Film. (n.d.-b). *Sarajevo UNESCO city of film*. https://sarajevocityoffilm.ba/sarajevo-unesco-city-of-film/

Sarajevo Film Festival. (n.d.). *Sarajevo film festival*. https://www.sff.ba/en

Semaine de la Critique. (2008). *Snijeg/snow*. https://www.semainedelacritique.com/en/edition/2008/movie/snijeg

Serbia Creates. (n.d.-a). *About us*. https://en.serbiacreates.rs/about-us-2/

Serbia Creates. (n.d.-b). *Creative industries*. https://en.serbiacreates.rs/creative-industries/

Shahidsaless, R., Blanco, F., Slavova, S., & Qorlazja, L. (2023). *Tourism 2.0 in Albania: A new opportunity for resilient growth*. World Bank Blogs. https://blogs.worldbank.org/en/europeandcentralasia/tourism-20-albania-new-opportunity-resilient-growth

Simjanovska, V. (2022). *Report on the impact of COVID-19 on the cultural and creative industries (CCIs) in North Macedonia*. Cultural Relations Platform. https://culturalrelationsplatform.eu/wp-content/uploads/2022/05/Report_CCIs-North-Macedonia-CRP-2022.pdf

Skampa International Theatre Festival. (n.d.). *Skampa international theatre festival*. https://www.skampafestival.com/

Sretenović, D. (2013). The political context of contemporary art production in Serbia. In A. Vujanović & B. Cvejić (Eds.), *Aesthetic education expanded* (pp. 112–125). kuda.org.

State Statistical Office of the Republic of North Macedonia. (2021a). *Census of population, households and dwellings in the Republic of North Macedonia, 2021: Book XIII*. https://www.stat.gov.mk/pdf/2021/3.1.21.14_mk.pdf

State Statistical Office of the Republic of North Macedonia. (2021b). *Census of population, households and dwellings in the Republic of North Macedonia, 2021: Book XIV*. https://www.stat.gov.mk/pdf/2021/3.1.21.15_mk.pdf

State Statistical Office of the Republic of North Macedonia. (2022). *Announcement no. 4.1.23.14* [Press release]. https://www.stat.gov.mk/PrikaziSoopstenie_en.aspx?rbrtxt=146
State Statistical Office of the Republic of North Macedonia. (2023). *North Macedonia in figures, 2023*. https://www.stat.gov.mk/publikacii/2023/Makedonijavobrojki2023ENweb.pdf
Statistical Office of the Republic of Serbia. (2022). *Statistical yearbook of the Republic of Serbia, 2022/Статистички годишњак Републике Србије, 2022*. https://publikacije.stat.gov.rs/G2022/pdf/G20222055.pdf
Statistical Office of Montenegro. (2023). *Culture and arts statistics 2019–2022*.
Statistical Office of Montenegro. (2024). *Population estimates and demographic indicators*. Retrieved July 4, 2025, from https://www.monstat.org/eng/page.php?id=23&pageid=23
Studio Kilica. (n.d.). *Studio Kilica*. https://www.studio-kilica.com/
Sunny Hill Festival. (n.d.). *About us*. https://sunnyhillfestival.com/about-us/
Svob-Đokić, N. (2005). Introduction. In N. Svob-Đokić (Ed.), *The emerging creative industries in Southeastern Europe* (pp. 1–3). Institute for International Relations. https://www.culturelink.org/publics/joint/cultid07/Svob-Djokic_Creative_Industries.pdf
Swisscontact. (2022). *Manifesta 14 transforms Kosovo's capital into a 100-day exhibition venue*. https://www.swisscontact.org/en/news/manifesta-14-transforms-kosovos-capital-into-a-100-day-exhibition-venue
Tanović, D. (Director & Writer). (2001). *No man's land* [Film]. Noé Productions; Fabrica Cinema; Man's Films; Counihan Villiers Productions; Studio Maj–Casablanca; Océan Films; Momentum Pictures; Minority co-producers.
Teatri Migjeni. (n.d.). *Teatri Migjeni Shkodër* [Migjeni theatre Shkoder]. https://teatrial.home.blog/teatri-migjeni-shkoder/
TERA Consultants. (2014). *The economic contribution of the creative industries to EU GDP and employment: Evolution 2008–2011*. https://www.teraconsultants.fr/wp-content/uploads/2014/10/2014-Oct-European-Creative-Industry-GDP-Jobs-full-Report-ENG.pdf
Throsby, D. (2008). The concentric circles model of the cultural industries. *Cultural Trends*, *17*(3), 147–164. https://doi.org/10.1080/09548960802361951
Tirana Times. (n.d.). *Tirana Times*. https://tiranatimes.com/?page_id=396&_s2member_vars=post.level.4.post.115421.. https://tiranatimes.com/?page_id=396&_s2member_vars=Lz9wPTExNTQyMQ%3D%3D&_s2member_sig=1729087508-d69b01be1a820ee2ab0bee0a79a4b12f
Tomka, G. (2016). *Audience is watching you: Challenges to audience development by independent cultural organisations in Bosnia and Herzegovina, Macedonia and Serbia*. Youth Cultural Center – Bitola.
Turp-Balazs, C. (2024). *Economy in focus: Kosovo*. Emerging Europe. https://emerging-europe.com/analysis/economy-in-focus-kosovo-2/
UNESCO. (2006). *Understanding creative industries: Cultural statistics for public-policy making*. https://www.americansforthearts.org/sites/default/files/pdf/2015/international/UNESCO_Understanding_Creative_Industries.pdf
UNESCO. (2020). *Quadrennial periodic report: Albania 2020*. https://media.unesco.org/sites/default/files/webform/dce002/QPR_2020_AL_0bcc58e0-7e22-4c50-a063-da08c9066c21_10.pdf

UNESCO. (2022). *Re|shaping policies for creativity: Addressing culture as a global public good; executive summary*. https://unesdoc.unesco.org/ark:/48223/pf0000380476

UNESCO Institute for Statistics. (2009). *2009 UNESCO framework for cultural statistics*. https://uis.unesco.org/sites/default/files/documents/unesco-framework-for-cultural-statistics-2009-en_0.pdf

UNICEF. (2023). *Bosnia and Herzegovina: Country office annual report 2023*. https://www.unicef.org/media/152011/file/Bosnia-and-Herzegovina-2023-COAR.pdf

United Nations. (2022). *Common country analysis update*. https://montenegro.un.org/sites/default/files/2022-12/Common%20Country%20Analysis%20Update%202022.pdf

United Nations Conference on Trade and Development. (2010). *Creative economy report 2010: Creative economy: A feasible development option*. United Nations Publications. https://unctad.org/system/files/official-document/ditctab20103_en.pdf

United Nations Conference on Trade and Development. (2024). *Creative economy outlook 2024: Technical and statistical report*. United Nations. Retrieved June 22, 2024, from https://unctad.org/system/files/official-document/ditc2024_en.pdf

United Nations Development Programme. (2023). *Hope for a more sustainable future in fashion in Kosovo*. https://www.undp.org/kosovo/stories/hope-more-sustainable-future-fashion-kosovo

United Nations Development Programme. (n.d.). *Creative industries project*. https://www.undp.org/kosovo/projects/creative-industries

United Nations Economic Commission for Europe. (n.d.). *Bosnia and Herzegovina: Country profile*. https://w3.unece.org/CountriesInFigures/en/Home/Index?countryCode=070

University of Belgrade, Faculty of Economics. (2022). *Assessment of the economic impact of the creative industries sector on the economy of the Republic of Serbia*. National Platform Srbija stvara/Serbia Creates.

University of Belgrade, Faculty of Economics. (2024). *Analiza ekonomskih efekata sektora muzičke industrije na ekonomiju Srbije* [Analysis of the economic impact of the music industry sector on the economy of Serbia]. Nacionalna platforma Srbija stvara/Serbia Creates. https://serbiacreates.rs/wp-content/uploads/2024/03/Muzicka-industrija-Report-2024.pdf

Vijesti. (2023). *The first Adria gaming conference starts tomorrow*. https://en.vijesti.me/fun/Gaming/667037/the-first-adria-gaming-conference-starts-tomorrow

Visit Tirana. (n.d.). *National gallery of arts*. https://www.visit-tirana.com/locations/national-gallery-of-arts/

The Work Foundation. (2007). *Staying ahead: The economic performance of the UK's creative industries*. The Work Foundation. https://static.a-n.co.uk/wp-content/uploads/2013/11/4175593.pdf

World Bank. (2021). *Bosnia and Herzegovina macro poverty outlook: Country-by-country analysis and projections for the developing world*. https://thedocs.worldbank.org/en/doc/d5f32ef28464d01f195827b7e020a3e8-0500022021/related/mpo-bih.pdf

World Bank. (2024a). *Kosovo overview*. https://www.worldbank.org/en/country/kosovo/overview

World Bank. (2024b). *Serbia overview*. https://www.worldbank.org/en/country/serbia/overview
World Bank Group. (2024a). *Western Balkans regular economic report no. 25, Spring 2024: Invigorating growth*. International Bank for Reconstruction and Development/The World Bank. https://documents1.worldbank.org/curated/en/099040524061582128/pdf/P5006481fb98fb0db1a9401e200293e761d.pdf
World Bank Group. (2024b). *Macro poverty outlook: Country-by-country analysis and projections for the developing world – Europe and Central Asia*. International Bank for Reconstruction and Development/The World Bank.
Žbanić, J. (Director & Writer). (2020). *Quo Vadis, Aida?* [Film]. Deblokada Film, Digital Cube, Coop 99, N279 Entertainment, Razor Filmproduktion, Extreme Emotions, Indie Prod.

3 Capacities in the Cultural and Creative Industries in the Western Balkans

What and How?

Human Capital

The Western Balkans at a Crossroads: Talent Migration and the Struggle to Retain Skilled Professionals

Human capital is an essential resource in the CCI, where value creation often depends on intellectual, creative, and artistic inputs from the individuals rather than just material resources. One of the most significant challenges to the human capital in the CCI sector in the Western Balkans region is the migration of talent and skilled professionals. This phenomenon significantly influences the development of these countries due to various historical, political, social, and economic factors. The Western Balkans has a long tradition of migration, particularly after the WWII, when many citizens sought to migrate to other countries and continents in search of a better future. The most desired destinations at that time were the USA, Australia, and Europe.

The conflict in the former Yugoslavia initiated the last strong wave of migration, as many individuals seeking a safe place to live sought asylum in various countries, primarily in Europe, but also in the USA, Australia, and some Arabic countries. This trend continued even after the conflict in 1990s, since all the countries of the Western Balkans started the process of EU integration. According to Icoski (2022) and Jovanovski (2024), the primary cause of the recent migration wave, which is still ongoing, is the youth's disillusionment with their future, and more importantly, their lack of trust in their countries' systems. Issues such as corruption, delayed reforms, economic stagnation, pollution, limited opportunities for progress, and the realisation of potential are the primary causes of this migration wave (Icoski, 2022; Jovanovski, 2024).

However, the citizens of the Western Balkans are not the only ones driving this migration phenomenon. The shifting demographics of the EU and the aging population in Europe as a whole, encouraged numerous decision-makers to develop strategies and instruments aimed at attracting young creative and talented individuals, who would remain in these countries and contribute to

DOI: 10.4324/9781032724669-4

their development. As a result, many young, well-educated, and creative individuals have left and are continuing to leave the region, seeking opportunities for their self-realisation and a better life, thereby contributing to the economic growth of those countries.

According to Icoski, the Western Balkan countries have lost approximately 20% of their population in the last 10 years, with Serbia losing 9%, North Macedonia 10%, Bosnia and Herzegovina 24%, and Albania 37%. The report indicates that the largest demographic among these figures consists of young, educated, and skilled individuals who have chosen to emigrate due to challenging political, social, and economic conditions, as well as due to the low level of quality-of-life (Icoski, 2022). This brain drain process is particularly evident in the education system across all countries, as it has resulted in a significant decrease in the number of pupils and students in recent years. It is also evident in the CCI sector, where many creative individuals are migrating abroad in search of a better future and are not returning to their country of origin. According to the same policy paper, the main desired destinations for young people are the EU, the UK, Australia, Canada, the USA, and Switzerland.

There is no simple answer for how to solve this issue. The migration of the best creative and intellectual human potential from the Western Balkans to other countries has a long-term negative impact on these countries. This trend affects not only the quality of education, science and research, and innovation, but also administration and politics. Many EU progress reports for the Western Balkans countries acknowledge the weakened human capacities in all these fields.

Several aspects suggest potential solutions to this issue within the context of the Western Balkan countries. First, this process can be seen not only through a negative perspective of brain drain but also as an opportunity to bring this potential back to the countries of origin and promote circular migration. For this scenario, the holistic approach needs to be adopted, with fostering strong regional cooperation, acceleration of the EU integration process, making a common policy for migration, and, of course, improvement of the life and working conditions of this potential and the inclusion of the diaspora in this process need to be adopted. Unfortunately, this scenario of accelerated development of the region and utilisation of all its potential, including the diaspora, in relation to the issue of brain drain at the time when this book is being developed, looks like utopia.

Education and Skills Gap

The Western Balkans (WB) region faces significant challenges in its CCI, particularly in terms of human resources' qualification, education, and skills. Despite its rich cultural history, educational institutions often fail to equip young professionals with the necessary knowledge and skills to succeed in local and global markets. According to PAC Multimedia's research on cultural skills and shortages in the Western Balkans (2018), graduates are underprepared for technical, creative, or business roles in the cultural sector. This inadequacy is compounded by outdated training programmes, limited opportunities for ongoing professional development, and underdeveloped infrastructure, particularly in rural areas. These factors constrain access to global markets and modern production tools, further limiting the potential of the region's creative industries (PAC Multimedia, 2018).

PAC Multimedia's research shows that a cross-analysis of skill gaps in the Western Balkans reveals that both transversal and technical skills are lacking across the cultural sector. More precisely, the most pressing skill shortages are in areas such as strategic planning, audience engagement, entrepreneurial skills, cultural management, fundraising, networking, and technical and digital skills. Specifically, there is a need for international exposure to best practices, with many young professionals seeking to gain experience abroad to fill these gaps. Senior professionals are also underqualified, lacking up-to-date skills in both cross-sectoral management and technical areas, such as lighting, sound design, and restoration. This lack of adequate training opportunities is a significant contributor to the brain drain phenomenon, mentioned previously, as many young professionals leave the region in search of better career prospects.

In parallel, OECD (2024) data highlight that the broader educational landscape in the Western Balkans also suffers from similar quality issues. According to this data, the 2022 Programme for International Student Assessment (PISA) revealed that 79% of the young population (up to 15 years old) in the Western Balkans had shown low performance in at least one subject, such as science, mathematics, and reading (OECD, 2024). According to Brajkovic (2023) and OECD & UNICEF (2022), by the age of 15, many students underperform in subjects such as mathematics and science, as seen in Serbia, Bosnia and Herzegovina, North Macedonia, and Kosovo. Furthermore, tertiary education in the region plays a crucial role in the broader EU accession goals but struggles with challenges such as knowledge gaps, low-quality teaching, and incomplete adoption of the Bologna Process, particularly in Kosovo. Limited reforms have negatively affected university rankings and skills gaps in the workforce (Brajkovic, 2023; OECD & UNICEF, 2022).

Compared to the EU average education spending, the Western Balkans it is 20% lower, with over 80% of the budget spent on salaries and very few investments in human capacities, technology, and other infrastructure. Skills intelligence systems are similarly underdeveloped, with irregular analyses and decentralised data collection further inhibiting efforts to address current and future skills needs (OECD, 2024).

The education systems in the Western Balkans, despite some progress in learning outcomes, face significant gaps, especially in foundational literacy and higher-order skills. Key areas for improvement include enhancing digital skills, transitioning to a green economy, tackling the out-migration of young talent, ensuring institutional governance, improving secondary vocational education (VET), and addressing inequality in educational outcomes (Brajkovic, 2023; OECD & UNICEF, 2022).

These challenges in the education system extend into the CCI sector, where a mismatch between the skills being taught and the actual need of the market is evident. Both young and senior professionals express dissatisfaction with the quality of education and training available to them. In addition, for young people entering the cultural sector, the lack of practical skills and hands-on experience is a significant barrier to success. At the same time, senior professionals are inhibited by a lack of opportunities for continuous professional development (PAC Multimedia, 2018; Simjanovska, 2022).

Unfortunately, the capacity building offers in the region are neither promising nor of high quality. Most of the region's public universities are outdated, lacking programmes tailored to the cultural sector's needs. Furthermore, the quality of education provided by majority of private universities in the Western Balkans countries is questionable, as their primary motivation for excellence is economic profit, which raises doubts about their relevance. Degrees from these institutions are often easy to obtain, with minimal academic efforts, and there are no effective instruments in place to control or ensure the quality of education. This situation worsens the concerns about the long-term value of the qualifications they offer and the competencies of their graduates.

One of the very few exceptions is the University of Arts in Belgrade, offering international programmes in CCI related fields, where students can get relevant knowledge and opportunity to enlarge the social network with international students. Unfortunately, the number of available places in this university is limited and many youngsters from the region are forced to go abroad to get proper education in this specific field. The current gap in comprehensive capacity-building programmes within the CCI sector is only partially addressed by initiatives from civil society organisations, strongly supported by the international community present in the region, such as the British Council, European Commission, and UNESCO. These organisations, such as Lokomotiva from North Macedonia, Hartefact Serbia, KotorArt Montenegro, ODA Theater Kosovo, etc., offer relevant, specialised short-term training programmes tailored to specific target groups, covering areas such as curatorial practices, strategic management in arts organisations, digital marketing, audience engagement, and branding, among others (PAC Multimedia, 2018).

This lack of strategic focus on capacity building in the CCI sector limits the region's ability to develop cohesive CCI' initiatives. The impact of these skill shortages and educational deficiencies has far-reaching consequences. As the OECD (2024) notes, the Western Balkans economies have made limited progress in engaging adults in lifelong learning, and participation rates in continuing education are half the EU average. This further constrains the ability of professionals to adapt to the constantly evolving demands of the cultural sector.

Addressing these skill gaps is crucial for the Western Balkans region's CCI to realise its full potential. The development of specialised education and training programmes, with a focus on both technical and transversal skills, is essential. Moreover, greater international collaboration, improved infrastructure, and enhanced language proficiency will play an important role in helping the Western Balkans creative industries thrive in the global market.

Institutional Capacities

In the Western Balkans, the political, social, economic, and cultural transitions, since the 1990s, have led to significant stagnation in terms of the institutional capacities of the CCI. The existing structures, management and decision-making mechanisms, financial capacities, and infrastructure are the main drivers of this sector and its development. Stagnation in any one of these factors has a significant effect on all others, ultimately impacting the entire sector. These challenges have created fragmented ecosystems where support for cultural development varies greatly. While some countries have made significant efforts in developing cultural policies, described in the previous chapters, the broader ecosystem remains fragmented, with institutions in some areas lacking the resources and capacity to effectively support the sector.

The CCI infrastructure in the Western Balkans (WB) is still developing, with both public and private initiatives contributing to its growth. Various creative hubs, such as Ložionica in Serbia (an old railway depot in Belgrade has been repurposed into a creative hub for various cultural and artistic activities (Lozionica, n.d.) and the Cerovo Regional Creative Hub in Montenegro (part of a broader initiative to reuse the Cerovo military complex, transforming it into a regional centre for innovation), are emerging as key spaces for innovation and creativity (United Nations Development Programme, n.d.). These hubs serve as a good example of physical venues where creative professionals and enterprises could interact, share ideas, and collaborate. However, challenges remain, particularly in terms of geographical distribution and access to resources. Creative clusters thrive in areas where local and regional authorities, business support agencies, and educational institutions intersect, providing an enabling environment for the CCI sector. Despite these efforts, gaps in infrastructure, particularly in rural or underdeveloped areas, hinder the sector's full potential (Cuff & Zečević, 2022).

Data Collection and Statistic Agencies

A fundamental barrier to the effective development of public cultural policies in the Western Balkans is the absence of comprehensive and reliable statistical data and the lack of research initiatives (Judah & Vracić, 2019). The responsible institutions for data collection and the statistical agencies in the region face serious challenges in collecting and analysing data related to CCI. Due to the multi-dimensional nature of culture, statistical classifications often vary, depending on the specific methodology used. For example, employment statistics require classifications of sectors and occupations, while trade statistics rely on goods and services categories (Simjanovska, 2022). Furthermore, in most of the Western Balkan countries, existing methodologies adhere to the NACE Rev. 2 classification, which tracks economic activities such as gross value added, gross income, and employment within the cultural sector. Despite the existence of a theoretical scope for cultural statistics, practical application can differ significantly between statistical domains. However, these statistics often fall short of international standards, failing to cover all subsectors within CCIs (OECD, 2024). Moreover, many of these agencies, including those in Bosnia and Herzegovina and Kosovo, collect data sporadically, which limits the ability of conducting vigorous policy evaluations.

In addition, comprehensive mapping of key players in the CCI sector is essential; however, it is still underdeveloped in most Western Balkan countries. For example, Albania, North Macedonia, and Serbia have made attempts to gather data on cultural actors, but these efforts remain fragmented and incomplete (OECD, 2024).

The lack of integrated and standardised data collection frameworks across the region remains one of the greatest barriers to developing comprehensive cultural policies. Without reliable data, it is challenging to measure the impact of policies and ensure the effective allocation of resources. Adopting frameworks like Eurostat or the 2009 UNESCO framework for cultural statistics could help standardise data collection across the region, providing a more accurate picture of the CCI sector's contributions to national economies.

However, there are promising developments that suggest a shift towards more structured and relevant research. One such example is the study by Cvetičanin et al. (2024), which proposes a unified research framework linking socioeconomic and digital inequalities in cultural participation. While not specifically focused on the Western Balkans, this type of research holds particular value for the region, where gaps in data and research are profound. The integrated framework presented in the study offers a tool that could guide both future research and policy development in the CCI sector, helping to address the very deficiencies that hinder effective cultural policy in the Western Balkans. By illustrating how to capture and interpret complex participation patterns, such initiatives provide a hopeful model for how evidence-based cultural strategies might evolve in the region.

Financial Capacity

Funding instruments play an important role in shaping the institutional capacity of the CCI sector, directly influencing its ability to prosper. The public funding for culture, in all Western Balkan Countries, is highly inconsistent. National institutions, such as Ministries of Culture in this region, often have limited resources and are primarily focused on their own agendas and priorities. This narrow approach can leave significant gaps, as these ministries may fail to address the broader and evolving needs of the CCI sector. The cultural budget allocated to these ministries is frequently inadequate, ranging from 0.7% to 1.5% when compared to the overall state budget. These limited funds further constrain the opportunities for development within the sector. According to Cuff and Zečević (2022), the range of financial commitments across the region in the CCI is relatively modest. Usually, the public institutions receive the majority of these available funds allocated to culture, whereas the CCI sector from the civil and private sectors receive very little.

The situation is further complicated by the gradual withdrawal of international donors following the onset of political transitions in the region. Moreover, the absence of individual and corporate philanthropy further limits alternative funding sources. The civil sector, often serving as a watchdog and ethical counterpart to governmental institutions, continues to face challenges in securing public funding. Despite its efforts, the civil sector rarely succeeds in developing sustainable strategies for self-financing, highlighting its dependence on public financial support.

In summary, the funding environment for CCIs in the Western Balkans remains precarious, with limited public resources, the declining presence of international donors, and a weak philanthropic culture posing significant barriers to sustainable growth in the CCI sector. Many organisations, individuals, and private companies in the region rely heavily on international donors, predominantly on European Union funding to sustain cultural initiatives, revealing a fragile funding ecosystem.

The Role of the European Commission

Following the conflicts in ex-Yugoslavia and the fall of the Communist regime in Albania, the process of EU integration has become crucial for all countries from the Western Balkans. The European Commission plays a significant role in all domains of this process, including the CCI. One of the most relevant instruments from the CCI sector is the Creative Europe programme (2014–2020), which allocated around €85 million to 230 cultural projects in the region. Furthermore, the same programme, which is budgeted at €2.44 billion for the period 2021–2027, fosters cultural cooperation and includes participation from the Western Balkans.

In 2021, the European Commission created a new initiative as part of the Creative Europe programme, providing €5 million to support 13 new Western Balkans projects (European Commission, 2024).

UNESCO, the British Council, and the Italian Agency for Development Cooperation are implementing the €8 million Culture and Creativity for the

Western Balkans (CC4WBs) programme, which the European Commission launched in 2022 and is focused on cultural heritage, artist mobility, and integrating vulnerable groups (European Commission, 2024).

Launched in 2023, the European Heritage Hub, with a €4.301 million budget for its pilot phase, aims to drive the digital transformation of heritage practices by April 2025, with Western Balkans countries participating in it (European Heritage Hub, n.d.-a, n.d.-b).

The EU's Instrument for Pre-Accession Assistance (IPA) serves as a crucial support system, fostering cooperation between the Western Balkans and the EU states. IPA III will receive €14.162 billion for the period 2021–2027. The cultural component of this instrument focuses on promoting cultural tourism and sustainable development (European Commission, n.d.).

According to Cuff and Zečević (2022), complementary programmes such as Horizon Europe, supporting innovation in the CCI sector, and Erasmus+, which enhances skills and mobility in the creative industries, are important mechanisms from which the CCI in the Western Balkans has benefitted. Another possibility is the European Investment Fund (EIF) and the Western Balkans Enterprise Development & Innovation Facility (WB EDIF), providing financial support to small and medium enterprises (SMEs) in the creative sector, with Western Balkans EDIF contributing €145 million in capital.

Despite the growing Euroscepticism in the Western Balkans, the EU, with all its instruments and financial mechanisms, remains the strongest supporter of the Western Balkans, contributing significantly to a broader social and cultural development.

References

Brajkovic, L. (2023). *Education policy and development in the Western Balkans*. European Association for International Education. https://www.eaie.org/resource/western-balkans-education-policy.html

Cuff, M., & Zečević, I. (2022). *Mapping of the creative industries in the Western Balkans*. Regional Cooperation Council. https://www.rcc.int/docs_archive?keyword=Mapping+of+the+creative+industries+in+the+Western+Balkans&search_category=0&date_from=&date_to=&last_id=0

Cvetičanin, P., Pereira, L. P., Petrić, M., Tomić-Koludrović, I., Lebaron, F., & Zdravković, Ž. (2024). Cultural practices and socio-digital inequalities in Europe: Towards a unified research framework in cultural participation studies. *Cultural Sociology*. Advance online publication. https://doi.org/10.1177/17499755231222520

European Commission. (2024). *EU and Western Balkans deepen cooperation on innovation, research, education, culture, youth and sport*. European Commission. https://ec.europa.eu/commission/presscorner/detail/en/ip_24_4983

European Commission. (n.d.). *Overview: Instrument for pre-accession assistance (IPA)*. https://neighbourhood-enlargement.ec.europa.eu/enlargement-policy/overview-instrument-pre-accession-assistance_en

European Heritage Hub. (n.d.-a). *Partners and funding: The European Heritage Hub is a pilot project funded by the European Union*. https://www.europeanheritagehub.eu/about-the-hub/partners-funding/#:~:text=The%20European%20Heritage%20Hub%20is,(90%25%20of%20total%20costs)

European Heritage Hub. (n.d.-b). *Where cultural heritage connects*. https://www.europeanheritagehub.eu/

Icoski, M. (2022). *Toward a new youth brain-drain paradigm in the Western Balkans*. German Marshall Fund of the United States. https://www.gmfus.org/sites/default/files/2022–08/A%20New%20Youth%20Brain-drain%20Paradigm%20in%20the%20Western%20Balkans.pdf

Jovanovski, B. (2024). Brain drain in Western Balkans spikes amid absence of opportunities. *Euronews*. https://www.euronews.com/my-europe/2024/09/16/brain-drain-in-western-balkans-spikes-amid-absence-of-opportunities

Judah, T., & Vracić, A. (2019). *The Western Balkans' statistical black hole*. European Council on Foreign Relations. https://ecfr.eu/article/commentary_western_balkans_statistical_black_hole_eu_enlargement/

Lozionica. (n.d.). *Lozionica*. https://www.lozionica.rs/

OECD. (2024). *Western Balkans competitiveness outlook 2024: Regional profile*. OECD Publishing. https://doi.org/10.1787/170b0e53-en

OECD & UNICEF. (2022). *The Western Balkans, Eastern Europe and Central Asia: Findings from PISA 2018 (highlights)*. UNICEF. https://www.unicef.org/eca/media/22081/file/PISA%20Highlights_final.pdf

PAC Multimedia. (2018). *Cultural skills research summary: Examining the cultural skills gaps and shortages in the Western Balkans*. British Council. https://www.britishcouncil.org/sites/default/files/h086_02_culturalskillsunit_western_balkans_final_web_1.pdf

Simjanovska, V. (2022). *Report on the impact of COVID-19 on the cultural and creative industries (CCIs) in North Macedonia*. Cultural Relations Platform.

United Nations Development Programme. (n.d.). *Innovation challenge to reuse the Cerovo military complex*. https://www.undp.org/montenegro/innovation-challenge-reuse-cerovo-military-complex

4 Current Issues in the CCI in the Western Balkans

The Importance of the Individual Efforts

In June 2024, *Financial Times* opened its web edition with the headline: "Balkan artists step into the spotlight" (Morelli, 2024). While Balkan art, as a whole, attracts attention during and after the conflict in ex-Yugoslavia in the 1990s, with exhibitions such as "Balkan Art generator" – part of Brussels Cultural Capital 2000 and coordinated by PAC Multimedia from Skopje (PAC Multimedia, 2000);[1] exhibition at the Centre Pompidou in Paris, such as *"Balkan Insight"* (Jusić, 2016),[2] and the exhibition "Ostalgia" in the New Museum in New York (New Museum, 2011),[3] etc., it still remains under-represented internationally. However, the region is positioned, largely dependent, and driven by the resilience and innovation of its individual creators.

Despite systemic challenges such as limited public funding, underdeveloped capacities and infrastructure, and inconsistent government support for cultural policies and practices, the Western Balkans is home to a wealth of creative talent. Artists, musicians, designers, filmmakers, and other cultural professionals from Western Balkans countries, are stepping forward with a clear vision and distinct creative voices. They are forced by a desire to transcend local limitations, taking ownership of their own narratives and bringing them to the international stage.

A recurring theme within the Western Balkans' creative industries is the importance of individual capacity, charisma, and vision. Much like the global art icon Marina Abramović, one of the few widely recognised artists from ex-Yugoslavia, many emerging creators from the region are cultivating unique personal brands that resonate beyond local borders. These individuals possess a rare combination of artistic talent, knowledge, experience, entrepreneurial drive, and cultural diplomacy skills, allowing them to navigate an often fragmented and complex ecosystem.

The strength of the Western Balkans' creative industries lies in these individual efforts. Artists and cultural professionals are developing innovative projects, internationally connected, and are often working on cross-disciplinary collaborations to amplify their reach. These efforts are driven not only by their

DOI: 10.4324/9781032724669-5

artistic vision but also by their capacity to lead change within their communities, inspire younger generations, and contribute to the broader cultural landscape.

Showcasing these practices, there are examples of Balkan creators who have succeeded in shaping their own artistic paths. These individuals face complex restrictions, including poor legal and legislative solutions in their countries, copyrights, and a dysfunctional system for the protection of those rights, insufficient financial resources, inadequately educated human resources, etc. However, those same individuals, who come from different disciplines and initiatives from Tirana, through Sarajevo, Belgrade, Pristina, Podgorica, and Skopje, show incredible perseverance, resourcefulness, adaptability, and charisma. Their ability to create new opportunities in almost impossible and turbulent conditions characterises the state of CCI in the Western Balkans in 2020s. It is these individuals, leaders of small and medium-sized organisations that position the Western Balkans as a cultural and attractive force on the rise. A study by Dimitra Gkitsa examines self-organised cultural initiatives, exemplify how local actors navigate and adapt to challenging environments, creating opportunities for artistic expression and community engagement despite limited resources (Gkitsa, 2024).

These mentioned individuals are not only artists but also cultural managers, diplomats, visionaries who represent the future potential of the region's creative industries. Exploring these good practices in more depth, it becomes evident that the strength of the CCI in the Western Balkans is a testament to the perseverance, talent, and vision of individuals determined to leave their mark on the global cultural stage.

These emerging opportunities and individual-driven initiatives are exemplified by several flagship events and institutions across the Western Balkans. These initiatives include already established festivals, innovation hubs, and cultural centres that showcase local creativity and its impact at local, regional, and global levels. These initiatives not only articulate local potential and creative ideas into well-produced events and cultural and artistic goods but also serve as platforms for fostering creativity, innovation, collaboration, and cultural diplomacy. Art House from Skadar, Albania; Sarajevo Film Festival from Bosnia and Herzegovina; ODA Theatre from Kosovo; Montenegrin Film Centre from Montenegro; OXO from North Macedonia; and Two Desperados from Serbia are just a few examples of how creative and cultural industries can survive and thrive in the face of counterproductive challenges.

Sarajevo Film Festival – Bosnia and Herzegovina

Sarajevo Film Festival,[4] founded in 1995 by Obala Art Centre, is an excellent example of the CCI in the Western Balkans and its power of vision, charisma, resilience, and cooperation. The birth of this brave idea occurred during the armed conflict in Sarajevo, when the city remained under siege and when citizens were confronted with various forms of violence. The purpose of the festival was not only to give hope to the citizens and encourage the revival of civil society, but also to maintain the city's identity as a cosmopolitan city, a city that brings together different cultures and religions, a city that has touched many souls with its immediacy, kindness, openness, beauty, creativity, and good humour, and a city that has been an inspiration for many artists and creatives.

Behind this initiative are individuals, like Mirsad Purivatra and his team, who managed to make a successful story out of this festival and carry forward the festival's legacy of excellence. The vision, the passion for film, the belief in the potential of Sarajevo, managed to transform the festival from a marginal small modest initiative into a globally relevant cultural institution. Slowly but surely, the festival has grown into a platform for filmmakers globally, creating an opportunity to showcase emerging talent from a region with a rich but complex history. The idea's growth would not have been possible without the crucial international support during its initial years of formation. The festival also attracted the attention of many film icons, such as Angelina Jolie, Robert De Niro, and Morgan Freeman. They not only paraded through the red carpet but also became real ambassadors of this festival, attracting a lot of attention and highlighting its cultural significance on global level.

The festival's focus on nurturing young filmmakers and building a bridge for regional film industries exemplifies its commitment to growth and collaboration. The other important aspect of this festival, woven into its vision from the very beginning, is the education and promotion of young filmmakers from the region. With an industry segment that fosters education and networking, the Sarajevo Film Festival has become a catalyst for the creative energy of the Western Balkans. It provides a space where ideas and projects can flourish, bolstered by the presence of both local and international professionals. Over 100,000 attendees each year engage with the festival's high-quality programming, which now sets new standards for festival organisation and film promotion in the region (Sarajevo Film Festival, n.d.-a).

One of the Sarajevo Film Festival's most transformative segments is its industry-focused platform, CineLink Industry Days, launched in 2003 (CineLink Industry days, n.d.). It encompasses a number of initiatives, including CineLink Co- Production Market, CineLink Work-in Progress and Talents in Sarajevo (in cooperation with Berlinale talents). Collectively, these initiatives function as incubators for emerging talent and co-production opportunities across Europe and the wider region. CineLink has been remarkably important in supporting films such as *Quo Vadis, Aida* (directed by Jasmila Žbanić, Bosnia and Herzegovina), which secured critical funding, partnerships and visibility, earning global recognition, including nomination for Academy Award (Oscar) in 2021 (Sarajevo Film Festival, n.d.-a). This film was nominated in the category of

Best International Feature Film at the 93rd Academy Awards (Academy of Motion Picture Arts and Sciences, 2021).

CineLink Drama is another initiative, introduced in 2016, that responds to the growing demand for regional TV series and is dedicated specifically to the development and promotion of high-quality scripted television projects from Southeast Europe (Cineuropa, 2024). Project such as *The Hollow* (Bosnia and Herzegovina) and *The Silence* (Croatia/Ukraine) are examples that benefited from visibility and support through this platform (CineLink Industry Days, n.d.).

A unique initiative worth mentioning is the Docu Rough Cut Boutique, which supports documentary filmmakers from the region in finalising their films and gaining international exposure. According to the Sarajevo Film Festival (n.d.-b), the Docu Rough Cut Boutique was established in 2010 and it is organised in three working modules: Sofia, Cluj, and Sarajevo. It culminates at the Sarajevo Film festival, where selected projects are presented to industry decision makers. Notable documentaries that have participated in the Docu Rough Cut Boutique include *City of the Sun* (Kokosalakis, 2017), The Other Side of Everything by Mila Turajlić (2017), winner of Best Film at IDFA, *The Magic Life of V* by Tonislav Hristov (2019), selected for the Sundance Film Festival competition, *Srbenka* by Nebojša Slijepčević (2018), awarded at Visions du Réel, *Bottlemen* by Nemanja Vojinović (2023), winner of the Heart of Sarajevo for Best Documentary, *Her Mothers* by Asia Dér and Sári Haragonics (Dér & Haragonics, 2020), presented at Hot Docs and many more.

The Sarajevo Film Festival remains relevant due to its diverse programming, continuous support of local and regional talent, and collaboration with global networks, serving as a bridge between Western Balkans and global film industries. It is a powerful platform for young creatives where they have a chance to show their storytelling, creativity, and have an opportunity for exchange of ideas with relevant film workers. It became much more than a film festival. It is a symbol that shapes the identity of the city, illuminating the spirit of Sarajevo and its people, while continuing to inspire young generations of film workers and public in Sarajevo, the Western Balkans, and worldwide. It became one of the most relevant engines for sustainable development of the CCI in the Western Balkans.

OXO[5] *– North Macedonia*

OXO is a cultural non-governmental organisation from North Macedonia, located in Skopje and Bitola, one of the first of its kind in the Western Balkans, which started working in 1998.

In the same period, the role of cultural independent and non-governmental organisations, such as OXO, has been extremely important in shaping the cultural landscape of North Macedonia during its democratic and socio-political and economic transition. In this, post-socialist society, where the state cultural

Figure 4.1 Prespav 1, OXO production

infrastructure faced challenges, these kinds of organisations filled the vacuum by fostering civic engagement, intercultural dialogues, and independent artistic expression. They often acted as catalysts for institutional reform and as incubators for creative entrepreneurship, playing a central role in developing the CCI in the country (Compendium of Cultural Policies and Trends, 2022).

In the late 1990s, OXO focus was on promoting social, cultural, and educational development of the young population, initiating significant multi-year projects in capacity building, and opening discussions on different important topics, such as environment, sustainability, and diversity. Over the years, this organisation has evolved, expanding its scope of work, including the production of documentaries, short films, and other audio/visual content, and growing into a creative hub where young, talented creatives and artists have the opportunity to articulate and realise their ideas and get the opportunity to mark themselves as part of the CCI's global market (OXO, n.d.-a).

Behind this whole idea stands Pece Taleski, a visionary and forward thinker, who founded this organisation with passion, knowledge, skill, and determination. OXO's journey showcases the importance of dedication, creativity, and leadership in a country and region where opportunities are very few. It has become a trailblazer in Macedonian media, pushing the boundaries of creativity in a challenging environment. The ability to create ecosystems that fuel the CCI has been central to OXO's important position.

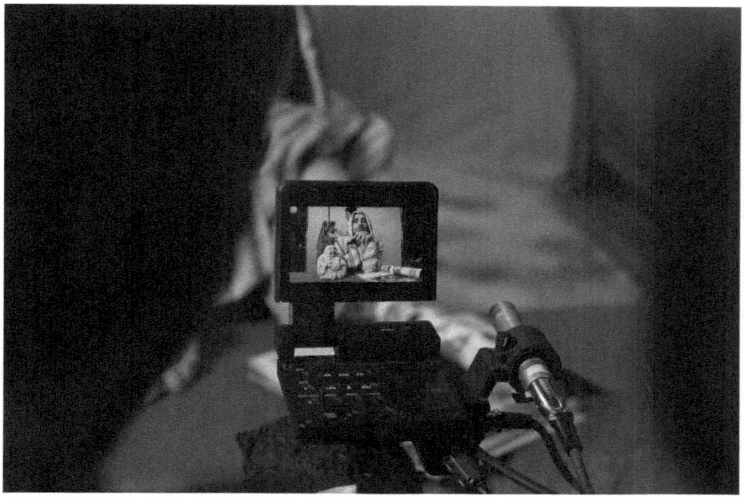

Figure 4.2 Prespav 2, OXO production

The projects initiated by OXO are more than productions; they integrate theatre, music, and marketing campaigns. This approach has helped it establish an enduring presence in the Macedonian cultural landscape. Among its notable productions are the educational children's programme 5+ Family, which not only entertains, but also fosters cultural dialogue and engagement (OXO, n.d.-b). In addition, its most notable achievement is the popular sitcom Prespav (2016–2022) (See the Figure 4.1, Figure 4.2 and Figure 4.3), co-produced with Macedonian National Radio Television (MRTV) and partially funded by the European Union. The series humorously addressed issues of identity, everyday politics, and European integration and was even featured in regional discussions on "TV diplomacy" due to its influence on intercultural understanding across the region (Okno.mk, 2022).

Its success led to a spin-off series, House Arrest (2022), further cementing OXO's status as a leader in domestic TV production (FilmNewEurope, 2022). The organisation also produced Radius, a bilingual documentary series that follows two young hosts from Macedonian and Albanian backgrounds, showcasing cultural heritage across the Balkans. This project, supported by the EU and aired on MRTV and Alsat, demonstrates OXO's ongoing commitment to intercultural dialogue and environmental awareness (TVpaket, 2023).

Beyond television, OXO's documentary portfolio includes *A Ton of Ice Cream, Solo Mode, We Are All Going to Die, and The Walk* – each presenting

Figure 4.3 Prespav 3, OXO production

unique stories of resilience, community, and humour in the face of adversity (Radiomof.mk, 2023; Makedox.mk, 2023).

One more successful project that they developed, "Gley," North Macedonia's first national streaming platform, is one of this organisation's most significant achievements. It elevates local production, offers a diverse range of high-quality domestic content, and opens up opportunities for international collaborations.

In development is another promising project, The Adventures of a Turbofolk Princess, a satirical TV series that was awarded major development grants at both the Sarajevo Film Festival and a Spanish co-production market (SDK.mk, 2023). This signals OXO's growing international recognition and its strategy of blending cultural critique with entertainment.

Over the past 25 years, OXO has demonstrated resilience, produced over 30,000 hours of content, and organising more than 150 concerts, live events, and theatre performances for children. This organisation demonstrates that financial resources do not define production quality. However, the current situation in North Macedonia, where financial resources are extremely limited presents a serious challenge. The organisation was compelled to make the most of its limited available budgets, find creative solutions, introduce new business models, and enhance its competitiveness in a broader context.

The crucial point for the development of OXO is forward-thinking leadership, a model that shows how to navigate local and global markets with detailed planning and adaptability.

OXO is a remarkable example of the CCI from North Macedonia, providing creative and innovative solutions, and serving as a creative hub for young talents entering the regional and global CCI market.

Two Desperados[6] *– Serbia*

Serbia is becoming one of the leading gaming industries in the Western Balkans, with the potential to compete on the global market.

Two Desperados is a company located in Belgrade and is one of the bright examples, which significantly contributes to the development of the CCI of Serbia. It was established in 2011, and one of the leading creative forces in that company was Marija Ilić, who was working in close collaboration with Vojislav Milutinović. Her vision and passion for Two Desperados is notable not only for successful games that have reached global proportions, but also for her commitment to gender diversity and inclusion. This company is a rare and good example in the world of games, in which the dominant population in the leading roles are men. It is breaking gender stereotypes and serving as an inspiration for a new generation of female leaders in the tech industry.

The company has gained international recognition primarily through its famous marble shooter games *Woka Woka* and *Violas Quest*, which count over 30 million of players globally (Google for Startups, n.d.). Key to their success is the user-oriented game design and content. Much of this success is attributed to the leadership's ability to integrate feedback from a broad and diverse player base, fostering continuous innovation.

Although the company's exact market valuation is not publicly disclosed, Two Desperados holds a competitive position in the casual gaming sector. According to the analytics platform Tracxn, it ranks 639th out of 8,532 companies in the casual mobile gaming space, alongside major industry players such as Zynga, Rovio, and Scopely (Tracxn, n.d.).

On the technological side, the company utilises Google's Firebase platform for analytics, A8B testing, remote configuration, and crash reporting. These tools help the team make informed decisions that enhance gameplay and improve user engagement (Google for Startups, n.d.).

Under the visionary guidance, Two Desperados has grown into a company of over 80 employees, with a focus on creating an inclusive workplace culture. Through platforms like Playroll, it has extended its hiring capabilities to countries such as France, Germany, UK, and Finland (Playroll, n.d.). Beyond its commercial achievements, the leadership's commitment to gender equality is reflected in the company's policies and its focus on promoting women in tech, positioning itself as a progressive employer in the Serbian and global gaming sectors (Two Desperados, n.d.).

Two Desperados continues to position itself as a leading example of creative innovation from the Western Balkans. Its ability to grow a global player base while remaining headquartered in Belgrade reflects its strategic vision and product excellence.

ODA Theatre[7] *– Kosovo*

The political and economic context of Kosovo over the past 25 years has contributed to a still-developing CCI sector. The war's aftermath, unresolved political status, and economic instability have created an environment in which cultural institutions often operate with limited support. However, several initiatives showcase the resilience and creative potential of Kosovo's CCI, with ODA Theatre (See Figure 4.4; Figure 4.5 and Figure 4.6) emerging as a prime example.

Founded in late 2002 by actor Lirak Çelaj and director Florent Mehmeti, ODA Theatre was established to provide a space for independent artistic expression during a time when Kosovo was still grappling with the refugee crisis and reconstruction. The theatre's first production, The Vagina Monologues, premiered on 1 March 2003, which has since been celebrated annually as its birthday (ODA Theatre, n.d.). This marked the beginning of its commitment to presenting bold and socially conscious work.

Figure 4.4 ODA Theater, Prishtina

Source: Photo by Atdhe Mulla. Courtesy of Kosovo 2.0

From its inception, ODA was envisioned as a platform to challenge traditional theatre by focusing on contemporary, multidisciplinary performances. According to Florent Mehmeti, the aim was to create "an independent theatre that would be flexible, adaptive and driven by artistic needs, not politics or bureaucracy" (Daku, 2023). This independence allowed ODA to serve as a dynamic space for cultural dialogue, resistance, and innovation.

ODA Theatre rapidly became one of the few multidisciplinary venues in Kosovo, combining theatre, performance, film, music, and visual art. By implementing this kind of activity, it became a cultural hub, attracting local, regional, and international artists. Beyond theatre performances, ODA supports the arts through concerts, exhibitions, and youth programmes, ensuring the cultivation of future artists. Its programming has consistently addressed pressing societal issues such as gender, ethnicity, corruption, and migration, making it a relevant and respected cultural actor. With more than 200 events annually and over 50,000 visitors each year, ODA functions as both a creative hub and a forum for civic discourse (ODA Theatre, n.d.).

Its relevance extends beyond the national stage. ODA has positioned itself within European theatre networks, including the Informal European Theatre Meeting (IETM), and frequently collaborates on international projects. These connections have helped boost Kosovo's visibility in European cultural circuits and enabled knowledge exchange and artistic mobility (ODA Theatre, n.d.; Daku, 2023).

Figure 4.5 Shef Lumturimi, ODA Theater production, 2025

Source: Photograph by Agon Mehmeti

Figure 4.6 "#Kufiri", ODA Theater Production, 2024

Source: Photo by Ideal Nrecaj. Courtesy of ODA Theater

One of the most significant artistic voices associated with ODA is playwright Jeton Neziraj, whose provocative and darkly comic works have premiered there. For instance, his play Negotiating Peace satirises the 1999 peace talks that ended the war in Kosovo, offering a biting commentary on international diplomacy and local complicity (Bajrami, 2022). The Guardian described Neziraj's work as "an intoxicating cocktail of farce and tragedy," reflecting the complexities of Kosovo's post-war society (Wintour, 2023).

Furthermore, ODA has prioritised youth engagement through educational and outreach programmes that empower young artists and provide professional development opportunities. As Mehmeti noted, "We don't just want to be a theatre; we want to be a space where the next generation of Kosovar artists feel they belong" (Daku, 2023). These efforts contribute not only to the sustainability of the institution itself but also to the broader development of Kosovo's cultural ecosystem.

Despite limited public funding and institutional support, ODA continues to thrive due to its adaptability, international partnerships, and visionary leadership. Its continued operation is a powerful example of how independent cultural institutions can play a crucial role in societal transformation, peacebuilding, and identity formation in post-conflict settings.

Film Centre of Montenegro – A Case of Public Sector

The Film Centre of Montenegro (n.d.), established in late 2016, represents a rare example of a structured and well-resourced public sector initiative aimed at revitalising a cultural and creative industry (CCI) in the Western Balkans. In the post-independence period, Montenegro's film sector faced significant challenges due to limited infrastructure, weak institutional memory, and a small domestic market. The establishment of FCMN under the leadership of Sehad Čekić was a strategic step towards centralising and professionalising national film policy (Cineuropa, 2017).

From its beginning, FCMN was modelled after successful regional and European examples. It manages the national film fund, supports domestic productions, promotes Montenegrin cinema abroad, and organises capacity-building initiatives. One of its major achievements is the launch of the "Film in Montenegro" incentives programme, offering a 25% cash rebate to attract foreign productions, a move designed to position the country as an attractive filming destination and support the local economy (European Film Commissions Network, n.d.).

International cooperation remains a cornerstone of FCMN's strategy. Its partnerships, such as the 2025 Memorandum of Cooperation with the National Film Centre of Moldova, show a commitment to regional integration and cross-border cultural diplomacy (Cineuropa, 2025). Under current director Aleksandra Božović, the Centre has also made notable efforts to support

Figure 4.7 © Film Centre of Montenegro, 2024

emerging filmmakers and promote gender inclusion, including a 2025 competition for women-led projects (FilmNewEurope, 2025).

Despite these successes, the Film Centre's identity as a state-run body also presents limitations. Public institutions, by their nature, are often constrained by bureaucratic processes, political expectations, and shifting ministerial agendas. Unlike independent cultural organisations, FCMN lacks the flexibility to rapidly respond to evolving artistic trends or urgent socio-political issues (Dragićević Šešić & Dragojević, 2005). Its programming and funding priorities can be slow to adapt, which may hinder experimentation and risk-taking, qualities that are essential in developing a vibrant and diverse film culture. Moreover, while the Centre has become a reliable promoter of Montenegrin film on the international stage, it still struggles with challenges common to public institutions in small states, such as limited human resources, over-centralisation of decision-making, and dependency on annual public funding allocations. These structural constraints can inhibit long-term planning and sustainability, especially in the face of changing political climates or budget cuts.

Nonetheless, initiatives like Montenegro Film Rendezvous and participation in Creative Europe's MEDIA subprogramme have demonstrated that even within a relatively rigid institutional structure, there is potential for innovation and network-building (FilmNewEurope, 2024). FCMN's ability to balance its administrative responsibilities with its artistic mission will be critical in ensuring that it continues to act not only as a cultural gatekeeper but also as an enabler of creativity.

In sum, while the FCMN is a commendable example of state investment in culture, it also illustrates the inherent tensions between institutional stability and artistic flexibility in the public administration of CCIs. Understanding these dynamics is essential for designing effective cultural policies that foster both excellence and diversity in small and emerging film industries.

Art House Albania[8]– Independent Cultural Innovation in Post-Transition Albania

In the post-socialist era, Albania's cultural infrastructure has undergone a difficult transformation. While the state retained a central role in institutional culture, independent initiatives have struggled to gain footing due to weak public funding, limited audience development, and infrastructural decay. However, in recent years, initiatives like Art House in Shkodër have begun to challenge these patterns, offering alternative modes of cultural production and rethinking the relationship between art, space, and community.

Founded in 2015 by internationally renowned artist Adrian Paci and his daughter Melisa Paci, Art House is a non-profit cultural space situated in the artist's childhood home. It functions both as a residency programme and as a gallery/exhibition space that promotes contemporary art, dialogue, and collaboration among local and international artists (Domus, 2019). The initiative

Figure 4.8 Art House. © Art House

is remarkable in the Albanian context, where few sustainable independent spaces for visual arts exist outside Tirana.

Art House has become a platform for artists to engage with contemporary themes such as displacement, identity, exile, and memory – issues that deeply resonate in Albanian society given its past under communist dictatorship and the mass emigrations of the 1990s. Adrian Paci's personal experience of migration and exile in Italy after the collapse of the Albanian regime shapes the ethos of the space. His multimedia practice – combining video, performance, and photography – attracts a younger generation of Albanian artists who find inspiration in his blend of the personal and the political (South of Imagination, 2021).

What sets Art House apart is its model of "situated" cultural practice. The decision to locate it in Shkodër – a northern city often overshadowed by the capital – reflects an intentional decentralisation of cultural activity. As Paci himself has noted, the idea was to "valorize the energy of the territory" and build cultural continuity in places historically neglected by national policy (Domus, 2019).

Art House also exemplifies the fusion of culture and tourism, positioning itself as a point of artistic pilgrimage. With its high-profile residencies, exhibitions, and discussions, it has become a cultural attraction that indirectly supports the local economy (South of Imagination, 2021). Yet, unlike more commercial art ventures, it remains rooted in critical inquiry, emphasising exchange over spectacle.

Still, the sustainability of Art House relies heavily on external funding, sporadic project grants, and the personal involvement of its founders. This underlines a broader challenge faced by independent cultural initiatives in the Western Balkans: they often operate in a vacuum of institutional support and policy frameworks that recognise their contributions. Moreover, without systematic national strategies for contemporary art or cultural decentralisation, such initiatives remain fragile, however impactful.

In summary, Art House stands as an important case of grassroots cultural infrastructure in Albania. It reveals how independent cultural actors can shape critical discourse, engage new audiences, and decentralise artistic production, even amid institutional constraints. It also illustrates the value of personal narrative and local place-making in constructing globally connected yet locally grounded artistic communities.

Notes

1 PAC Multimedia. (2000). *Balkan art generator exhibition*. https://www.basis-wien.at/db/event/65888%3Bjsessionid%3DA600C6F76BAF725C5E88C35866B49D5E?wicket%3ApageMapName=orgWitzmann&utm_source=chatgpt.com
2 Jusić, A. (2016, April 25). *Balkan Insight @ Centre Pompidou*. https://adelajusic.wordpress.com/2016/04/25/balkan-insight-centre-pompidou
3 New Museum. (2011). *Ostalgia*. https://archive.newmuseum.org/exhibitions/1394
4 Sarajevo Film Festival. (n.d.-b). *Sarajevo film festival*. https://www.sff.ba/en
5 OXO. (n.d.). *Association for education, communication and consulting*. https://oxo.mk
6 Two Desperados. (n.d.). *Official website*. https://twodesperados.com
7 ODA Theatre. (n.d.). *Homepage*. https://teatrioda.com/en/homepage/
8 Art House Albania. (n.d.). *Art house: Where art lives*. https://arthouse.al/?lang=en

References

Academy of Motion Picture Arts and Sciences. (2021). *The 93rd academy awards: Nominees and winners*. https://www.oscars.org/oscars/ceremonies/2021

Art House Albania. (n.d.). *Art house: Where art lives*. https://arthouse.al/?lang=en

Bajrami, B. (2022). Kosovo theatre showcase 2022: A platform for collaboration. *SEEstage*. https://seestage.org/features/kosovo-theatre-showcase-2022-collaboration/

CineLink Industry Days. (n.d.). *CineLink drama*. https://www.cinelinkindustrydays.com/

Cineuropa. (2017). *Montenegro establishes film centre.* https://cineuropa.org/en/newsdetail/321393/

Cineuropa. (2024). *Sarajevo rounds off this year's CineLink drama selection.* https://cineuropa.org/en/newsdetail/462436/

Cineuropa. (2025). *The film centres of Montenegro and Moldova sign collaboration agreement.* https://cineuropa.org/en/newsdetail/474272/

Compendium of Cultural Policies and Trends. (2022). *North Macedonia country profile.* https://www.culturalpolicies.net/database/search-by-country/country/north-macedonia/

Daku, F. (2023). Teatri ODA at 20: The journey of an independent theatre in Kosovo. *SEEstage.* https://seestage.org/interview/oda-theatre-20-independent-kosovo/

Dér, A., & Haragonics, S. (Directors). (2020). *Her mothers* [Film]. Campfilm. https://cineuropa.org/film/387853/

Domus. (2019). *Adrian Paci's art house, deeply-rooted in the local territory, is a residence that valorises cultural energy.* https://www.domusweb.it/en/art/2019/03/29/adrian-pacis-art-house.html

Dragićević Šešić, M., & Dragojević, S. (2005). *Arts management in turbulent times: Adaptable quality management.* European Cultural Foundation.

European Film Commissions Network. (n.d.). *Spotlight on: Film centre of Montenegro.* https://eufcn.com/spotlight-on-film-centre-of-montenegro/

Film Centre of Montenegro. (n.d.). *Film centre of Montenegro official website.* https://fccg.me/en/

FilmNewEurope. (2022). *House arrest: New Macedonian TV series by OXO.* https://www.filmneweurope.com/news/macedonia-news/item/123923-production-oxo-debuts-macedonian-tv-series-house-arrest

FilmNewEurope. (2024). *Montenegro film Rendezvous – a new initiative by film centre of Montenegro.* https://filmneweurope.com/press-releases/item/126068-montenegro-film-rendezvous-a-new-initiative-by-film-centre-of-montenegro

FilmNewEurope. (2025). *Montenegro launches script development and project development competitions for female filmmakers.* https://www.filmneweurope.com/news/montenegro/item/126676-montenegro-launches-script-development-and-project-development-competitions-for-female-filmmakers

Gkitsa, D. (2024). Grassroots creativity in arts and culture: A comparative analysis of case studies from the Balkans. *Creative Industries Journal, 17*(2), 234–253. https://www.tandfonline.com/doi/full/10.1080/17510694.2024.2363693

Google for Startups. (n.d.). *Two Desperados: Building a game studio in Serbia.* https://startup.google.com/alumni/stories/two-desperados/

Hristov, T. (Director). (2019). *The magic life of V* [Film]. Making Movies Oy. https://www.makingmovies.fi/portfolio/the-magic-life-of-v/

Jusić, A. (2016). *Balkan Insight @ Centre Pompidou.* https://adelajusic.wordpress.com/2016/04/25/balkan-insight-centre-pompidou/

Kokosalakis, R. (Director). (2017). *City of the sun* [Film]. Kolmo Films. https://www.berlinale.de/en/archive-selection/archive-2017/programme/detail/201703238.html

Makedox.mk. (2023). *The walk by Tamara Kotevska*. https://makedox.mk/mk/filmovi/patuvanje-pesh/

Morelli, N. (2024). Balkan artists step into the spotlight. *Financial Times*. https://www.ft.com/content/9c2e7d22–142a-43fe-b96e-af675717a73b

New Museum. (2011). *Ostalgia*. https://archive.newmuseum.org/exhibitions/1394

ODA Theatre. (n.d.). *About us*. https://teatrioda.com/en/about-us/

Okno.mk. (2022). *TV diplomacy in the Balkans*. https://okno.mk/node/88002

OXO. (n.d.-a). *About OXO*. https://oxo.mk

OXO. (n.d.-b). *OXO Macedonia*. https://oxo.mk/

PAC Multimedia. (2000). *Balkan art generator exhibition*. https://scca.ba/exhibitions/balkan-art-generator-exhibition/

Playroll. (n.d.). *Case study: Two Desperados*. https://www.playroll.com/case-studies/two-desperados

Radiomof.mk. (2023). *We are all going to die – tragicomic documentary*. https://www.radiomof.mk/site-kje-umreme-tragikomichen-dokumentarec-za-grobarskiot-biznis-vo-shtip/

Sarajevo Film Festival. (n.d.-a). *Industry platform overview*. https://www.sff.ba/en/page/industry

Sarajevo Film Festival. (n.d.-b). *Sarajevo film festival*. https://www.sff.ba/en

SDK.mk. (2023). *Avanturite na edna turbofolk princeza wins funding in Spain*. https://smart.sdk.mk/zhivot/tv/oho-dobi-50-iljadi-evra-na-festival-vo-shpanija-za-razvoj-na-tv-serijata-avanturite-na-edna-turbofolk-printseza/

Slijepčević, N. (Director). (2018). *Srbenka* [Film]. Restart. https://croatian.film/en/films/23508

South of Imagination. (2021). *From private to public: Adrian Paci and art house*. https://southofimagination.org/conversation/from-private-to-public-adrian-paci-and-art-house-2021/

Tracxn. (n.d.). *Two Desperados company profile & funding*. https://tracxn.com/d/companies/two-desperados/__2f4Itf91SDE3mMbhipPkAcZGyzT7ojNVuG1a5Q9zGOk

Turajlić, M. (Director). (2017). *The other side of everything* [Film]. Dribbling Pictures. https://www.idfa.nl/en/film/fe254d7d-1a18–4ff5-a5ae-90bfb0a58857/the-other-side-of-everything

TVpaket. (2023). *Radius – a docuseries on cultural heritage*. https://www.tvpaket.com.mk/stojanovska-i-vejseli-vo-doku-serijata-radius-na-mrt-1-i-alsat

Two Desperados. (n.d.). *Two Desperados: Game development company in Belgrade*. https://www.twodesperados.com/

Vojinović, N. (Director). (2023). *Bottlemen* [Film]. https://cineuropa.org/en/video/447831/

Wintour, P. (2023). Vain generals, mix-ups and Elvis: Kosovan play turns peace talks into farce. *The Guardian*. https://www.theguardian.com/world/2023/oct/27/vain-generals-mix-ups-and-elvis-kosovan-play-turns-peace-talks-into-farce

5 The Future of Cultural and Creative Industries in the Western Balkans

Final Remarks

As described in the previous sections of the book, CCIs in the Western Balkans have a turbulent past, shaped by complex social-political-economic and cultural dynamics. After the turbulent and conflict period in the region, in the 1990s, and the change of the political system, from socialism in ex-Yugoslavia and communism in Albania, to the transition towards neoliberal capitalist societies, CCIs emerged from grassroots initiatives (Biberaj, 2019; Prifti, 1978) in a very complex environment. Political elites and decision-makers did not, and in some countries still do not, have the capacity to recognise and provide some strategic directions for the development of this sector (Cuff & Zečević, 2022; Primorac, 2014; Cvetičanin & Bliznakovski, 2023).

Adding to this complexity, the developmental limitations of CCIs in this region are not solely institutional. According to Cvetičanin and Bliznakovski (2023), access to resources and opportunities is shaped not only by formal frameworks but also by societal norms and informal practices rooted in long standing clientelist networks. In other words, those with close ties to the political elites, often through nepotism, are more likely to secure public funds, while others struggle to receive any support. These "captured societies," as these authors call them, may inhibit innovation and reinforce inequalities within the cultural field. Thus, reform efforts should go beyond state policy and tackle broader socio-cultural dynamics that impact the cultural and creative eco system.

At the same time, independent cultural workers, CCI, and informal networks have been instrumental in shaping the cultural policy and practice in the region (Cvetičanin, 2011). Their adaptability, flexibility, participatory, and community driven approaches offer valuable models for inclusive and sustainable cultural development. Recognising and integrating these actors into policy frameworks could bridge gaps between formal institutions and vibrant grassroots initiatives, offering a more holistic and context-sensitive approach to the future of CCI sector.

Despite the lack of institutional recognition, charismatic individuals, mentioned in the previous chapter, initiated significant transformative cultural

DOI: 10.4324/9781032724669-6

activities and events. These cultural workers as well as several artists, musicians, filmmakers, and workers worked hard to rebuild their communities and cultural identity, and at the same time they have built bridges of regional and international connection. This impulse for creative action and resilience was not only about making art but worked in a wider context in terms of reconciliation, conflict resolution, solidarity, but also resistance in difficult times in the post-conflict transition, as exemplified in Serbia (Simjanovska, 2022).

The main generators for this incentive are individuals, non-governmental, and private and some public organisations, who deeply and firmly believed in the transformative power of culture and art and who possessed vision, knowledge, and good international connections.

Unfortunately, their relevance was much more recognised outside the borders than in their countries. The support they received and still receive from public institutions is minimal and insufficient.

After the end of this turbulent period in the 1990s, there comes a period of new opportunities. The EU integration is one of the most significant processes in the region that directly affects the development of CCI in this region, with specific and concrete financial assistance and the opportunity for collaboration within European networks. In addition, other international support is still present, such as the British Council, the UNESCO, USA programmes, which are stimulating this CCI development process. Thus, many festivals and events in music and performing arts, film, and in recent years the gaming industry, grow into significant cultural hubs, attracting domestic and foreign audiences (British Council, 2010; European Commission, n.d., 2024; UNESCO, n.d.)

Several festivals and creative hubs, ranging from film to music and game development, have flourished in recent years, increasingly attracting regional and international attention (Cuff & Zečević, 2022; Morelli, 2024). Events such as DokuFest in Prizren, Sarajevo Film Festival, Youth Theater Festival in Skopje, BITEF in Belgrade have become crucial platforms for regional expression and cross-border collaboration (GAP Institute, 2012; Sarajevo Film Festival, n.d.). The gaming industry in Serbia, also growing field in other Western Balkans countries, demonstrates significant potential for development of these countries (All Correct games, n.d.; British Council, 2022).

However, despite all the progress, there are still big challenges holding the sector back. An underdeveloped and fragmented infrastructure, lack of access to bigger markets, lack of adequate skills, and in general, the absence of relevant and coordinated policies and strategies between public and private sectors have affected the full potential of the CCI (OECD, 2024). Another important aspect is the regional (Western Balkans) cooperation, which is still underdeveloped in terms of infrastructure.

The creative industries in the Western Balkans are currently standing at a critical point. It can either grow significantly or face decline. Looking to the first scenario, the road ahead looks challenging; however, the light at the end of the tunnel is visible. CCIs in the Western Balkans have a bright perspective, primarily based on the existing creative potential that can be developed and become a part of the global creative world. However, for this scenario to come true, several important preconditions are needed. The key priorities should be securing a political will, then focus on research-based strategies with interdisciplinary approaches, investing in education and capacity building, as well as embracing technology and sustainability as core concepts and principles. If these approaches are accepted as basic principles for the development of industries in the region, they could become engines of innovation, social well-being, economic growth, and international presentation and recognition. This can turn the creativity into a legacy that will last for future generations. It would also help to change the perspectives and understanding of the region's rich cultural diversity, opening up the opportunity to share a new vision and perception of the Western Balkans with the rest of the world.

Looking forward, by formalising partnerships and fostering a broader understanding of the CCI sector, the region could develop a more coherent and sustainable creative ecosystem. Strengthening regional cooperation is crucial to making the creative industries more competitive. The Western Balkans could benefit from building cultural networks, pooling resources on a regional level (Western Balkans), and co-producing creative works that showcase the shared heritage and diversity of the region. Working together can help in leveraging the strengths and better positioning the region in the global creative economy. Some of the key steps to get there include raising the awareness of the region's creative potential, aligning with European and international best practices, and building platforms that bring stakeholders together. Additionally, targeted events that combine creative showcases with business knowledge and partnership building would help both the regional and the international collaboration.

Another important developmental aspect of the CCI is the education and human capacity building. There is an urgent need for re-shaping the existing educational programmes and perhaps the established new ones that will enforce the creative, communication, entrepreneurial, organisational and cultural management, research and analytical, technical production, and legal and ethical competences. A 2018 British Council report on cultural skills in the region identified major skills gaps in cultural management, production, and audience development (PAC Multimedia, 2018). Education reforms should also emphasise interdisciplinarity and foster collaboration between arts, technology, and entrepreneurship (OECD& UNICEF, 2022). Such alignment would prepare future professionals for a rapidly changing creative economy that increasingly realised on digital and cross-sector skills. By investing in all this, the cultural workers will be able to grow and be part of the global scene and market. Developing and adopting contextualised concepts and new models (business) for CCI, creating more opportunities for networking and mobility, could support these capacity-building efforts.

In addition, addressing the brain drain phenomena in the Western Balkans countries, could help in creating better working conditions for artists and cultural practitioners, and empower the human capital (Jovanovski, 2024; Icoski, 2022). Many skilled cultural workers, artists, and creative professionals leave the region in search of better opportunities. Tackling this requires systematic reforms in employment policies and incentive mechanisms that encourage talent retention. Providing sustainable career pathways and fair working conditions would foster human capital development.

Cultural policy reforms are also a key factor in unlocking the sector's potential (Simjanovska, 2022). Strategic initiatives that promote CCI as a driver for sustainable development and encourage regional and international collaboration would have a positive impact. A precondition to these policy reforms is having relevant research and data collection. The research field needs to be enforced and developed to have a clearer understanding of the needs and potential of the sector.

Other important aspects of the development of the CCI are digitalisation and sustainability.

Digital platforms offer incredible opportunities for artists, cultural organisations, and creative businesses to extend their reach far beyond local audiences (UNESCO, 2006, 2020). Digitalisation can enhance the visibility of creative outputs from the Western Balkans, provide access to a global audience, and enable cross-border collaborations without the usual limitations. Supporting these kinds of digital platforms, also integrating smart business models into the CCI ecosystem, could bring the resources together, connect stakeholders, generate new initiatives, and present the region's talent and potential on a wider scale (UNCTAD, 2022).

Moreover, sustainability, whether it is environmental, social, or economic, is not an option anymore. It should be at the heart of the plans for development of the CCI. The participants in the CCI sector need to be empowered to generate and drive relevant social and environmentally friendly practices that can also influence the wider communities. Supporting and implementing this kind of practice in the design and execution of festivals, events, performances, and creative production can bring tangible results, such as reducing ecological footprints and aligning the region with global sustainable trends. This approach can also be applied to the cultural heritage field, promoting sustainable tourism, relevant to the Western Balkans and in particular to Montenegro and Albania (Shahidsaless et al., 2023). Social sustainability should also be enforced, and that could strengthen the still fragile relationships between diverse communities and contribute to the well-being of the citizens living in these communities. Last, but not least important, economic sustainability could be reached by building resilient business models based on strong financial management models, diversifying income streams, reducing dependence on donor funding, and encouraging self-sustaining initiatives (UNCTAD, 2022).

Incorporating digitalisation and sustainability will not just modernise the sector, it will also provide long-term stability and growth. By combining these forces, the Western Balkans can become a vibrant hub for creative industries.

Conclusion

The CCI in the Western Balkans, although facing significant challenges in terms of politics, infrastructure, and regional and international connectivity, has a huge growth potential. The talent, passion, and resilience in these countries are an undeniable fact.

There is a strong belief that only by great investments and achieving excellence in the education and cultural sector, the Western Balkans can achieve rapid progress. The question is how to achieve this goal.

Securing strong political will for supporting CCI, promoting sustainable leadership, promoting cross-border and international cooperation, focusing on research- and data-based polices, investing in education, interdisciplinarity, radical inclusion, and bringing digitalisation and sustainability as key principles in every single CCI initiative will be a key in developing the existing potential in the CCI in the Western Balkans.

This vision looks beyond reach, yet with the right course, it could be navigated into the reality of tomorrow.

References

All Correct Games. (n.d.). *The Balkan gaming market*. https://allcorrectgames.com/insights/the-balkan-gaming-market/

Biberaj, E. (2019). *Albania in transition: The rocky road to democracy*. Routledge.

British Council. (2010). *Creative industries mapping in the Republic of Macedonia*. https://oer.makingprojects.org/creativemappingmacedonia.pdf

British Council. (2022). *Mapping the game development industry in Macedonia*. https://magda.org.mk/mapping-the-game-development-industry-in-macedonia

Cuff, M., & Zečević, I. (2022). *Mapping of the creative industries in the Western Balkans*. Regional Cooperation Council.

Cvetičanin, P. (2011). Non-institutional agents of cultural policy in Serbia, Montenegro and Macedonia. *Kultura*, *132*, 142–159.

Cvetičanin, P., & Bliznakovski, J. (2023). Captured states and/or captured societies in the Western Balkans. *Southeast European and Black Sea Studies*, *23*(1), 1–19. https://doi.org/10.1080/14683857.2023.2170202

European Commission. (2024). *EU and Western Balkans deepen cooperation*. https://ec.europa.eu/commission/presscorner/detail/en/ip_24_204

European Commission. (n.d.). *Overview: Instrument for pre-accession assistance (IPA)*. https://neighbourhood-enlargement.ec.europa.eu/instrument-pre-accession-assistance-ipa_en

GAP Institute for Advanced Studies. (2012). *The economic impact of DokuFest*. Institute for Advanced Studies GAP.

Icoski, M. (2022). *Toward a new youth brain-drain paradigm in the Western Balkans*. German Marshall Fund.

Jovanovski, B. (2024). Brain drain in Western Balkans spikes as new wave of youth leave region. *Euronews*. https://www.euronews.com/2024/02/21/brain-drain-in-western-balkans-spikes-as-new-wave-of-youth-leave-region

Morelli, N. (2024). Balkan artists step into the spotlight. *Financial Times*.

Organisation for Economic Co-operation and Development. (2024). *Western Balkans competitiveness outlook 2024: Regional profile* (Competitiveness and Private Sector Development). OECD Publishing.

Organisation for Economic Co-operation and Development, & United Nations Children's Fund. (2022). *The Western Balkans, Eastern Europe and Central Asia: Findings from PISA 2018 (Highlights)*. OECD Publishing; UNICEF.

PAC Multimedia. (2018). *Cultural skills research summary*. British Council.

Prifti, P. R. (1978). Socialist Albania since 1944: Domestic and foreign developments (Studies in Communism, Revisionism, and Revolution, Vol. 23). MIT Press.

Primorac, J. (2014). *The position and perspectives of cultural and creative industries in Southeastern Europe* [Položaj i perspektive kulturnih i kreativnih industrija u Jugoistočnoj Europi]. *Medijska istraživanja*, *20*(1), 45–65.

Sarajevo Film Festival. (n.d.). *Sarajevo film festival*. https://www.sff.ba/

Shahidsaless, R., Blanco, F., Slavova, S., & Qorlazja, L. (2023). *Tourism 2.0 in Albania: Creating jobs and opportunities for the next generation*. World Bank Blogs. https://blogs.worldbank.org/europeandcentralasia/tourism-20-albania-creating-jobs-and-opportunities-next-generation

Simjanovska, V. (2022). *Report on the impact of COVID-19 on the CCIs in North Macedonia*. Cultural Relations Platform.

UNESCO. (2006). *Understanding creative industries: Cultural statistics for public policy*. https://unesdoc.unesco.org/ark:/48223/pf0000147479

UNESCO. (2020). *Quadrennial periodic report: Albania 2020*. UNESCO.

UNESCO. (n.d.). *Culture and creativity for the Western Balkans (CC4WBs)*. https://www.unesco.org/en/cc4wbs

United Nations Conference on Trade and Development. (2022). *Creative economy outlook 2022: The International Year of Creative Economy for Sustainable Development – Pathway to resilient creative industries*.

Index

Note: Page numbers in *italics* indicate a figure, and page numbers in **bold** indicate a table on the corresponding page.

FSC
www.fsc.org
MIX
Papier | Fördert gute Waldnutzung
FSC® C083411

Kolibri 360 GmbH
Ferdinand-Jühlke-Straße 7
99095 Erfurt, Deutschland
produktsicherheit@kolibri360.de